INDIAN WOMEN: STRUGGLED LEGACY AND REALITY

SOCIAL ISSUES

JOINTLY AUTHORED BY- DR. JAYA BHARTI & DR. HITAISHI SINGH

"ALL AMAZING WOMEN WHO STRUGGLED TIRELESSLY BEARING ALL KINDS OF HUMILIATION TO ENSURE DIGNITY AND THE RIGHTFUL RIGHTS OF WOMEN"

Contents

Contents

Foreword

Indian women were never weak, neither in ancient nor modern times. On the contrary, she has always created a space for herself and made a path for self-development with her strong will and uncompromising zeal to move ahead. She exceeded all the adversities, using her practical insight and ingenious imagination, braving all difficulties with grit.

She took an active part in India's freedom struggles and today remains no less in any field. Like any multicultural and pluralistic society, India has also seen ups and downs since antiquity, and so is the status of Indian women. Therefore, the reforms and affirmative actions proved insufficient to address their concerns and issues. It gives me immense satisfaction to introduce **"Indian Women: A Struggled Legacy and Reality"** which is an honest attempt by the author duo- Dr. Jaya Bharti and Dr. Hitaishi Singh to analyze and bring forth the past struggles, current situation, and aspirations of women in India. Moreover, it discusses a host of women's issues in diverse circumstances and from various places, especially in the Indian subcontinent. Overall, this is a well-organized book that tries to give an in-depth understanding of the past scenario and gives direction to what is to be done for women's equality.

I congratulate both authors for bringing up much-needed resources in the domain of women's struggle. I recommend this book to all policy planners and other social sector professionals, academicians, research scholars, senior researchers, and students of women studies, social sciences, and other allied fields.I extend my best wishes for their future academic endeavors.

Rashmi Sinha
Former State Project Director, Mahila Samakhya, Uttar Pradesh.

Preface

"Freedom cannot be achieved unless the women have been emancipated from all forms of oppression."

Nelson Mandela

Indian women have progressed and traveled a long path of struggle to reach this destination. For the last 75 years (though they got the right to vote in 1935) Indian women have been participating and making strides steadily in the country's affairs. Their capability to adapt to new ways of life easily is a story to commend. They are gradually, sustainably, and increasingly venturing into new spheres of public and private sector jobs as well as handling their home fronts successfully. They are executing their roles with maturity, responsibility, and confidence and hence becoming high performers. They can be seen everywhere from grass root to the top level of authority with high proficiency. There have been women as President and Prime Minister of the country, they are being Governors, ministers, ambassadors, administrative officers, educationists, judges, bus and railway engine drivers, CEOs of multinationals, bankers, doctors, engineers, defense officers, fighter pilots, and the list is long. You name one and will find a woman on the list. Today there is no area left where they have not entered and made a mark.

But then a question arises......Did they reach the destination they and their predecessors strived for? It is a hard question to which we need an answer. In one frame there seems to be a rosy picture painted where women are seen as those fortunate ones who have achieved a great deal. They have the right to franchise, so they can vote; they have legal rights through which they can act in case of any discrimination or atrocity; abortions have been legal for many years now and sex-selective abortions have been banned for quite some time; they can aspire or be elected to any office in the country that men have access to and they can choose any job of their choice claiming equal salary as their male counterpart gets. Yet in another frame they found themselves trapped in many stereotype roles and category works. There are, within this gigantic framework, a million other contradictions and anachronisms which are extremely diverse, complex, and turbulent.

When we count the achievers, there is a visible wide gap. These achievers are fistful as compared to the majority group. Millions are still deprived of the basic right to life, to live a dignified life, to get proper shelter and secured safe life, to enter formal schooling, to have three full meals a day, to enjoy their childhood, to have access to safe water and get health facilities. These are just a few out of an array of problems women still face every day, every moment, and every bit of their life. The whole process of socialization and upbringing moulds her in such a way that she hardly gets a chance to think and act independently. The prime problems women face in India are really the problems of the whole country or you can say the whole women folk irrespective of any class or category. It is all-pervasive across religions, cast, and even socio-economic backgrounds barring a few exceptions.

On one hand, it appears that everything has been done for women if we consider the statuary and constitutional provisions. Yet there is a social tumult in the air, which is evident and is not underneath any layer. Paradoxically, the mindset of society at large is the decisive factor not the legal or constitutional framework in the Indian social predicament. Traditional attitudes of men and women, rigid customs, wilful denials of human rights still beset the masses of women, and the reformative acts remain just a piece of paper. The problem of Indian women is unique within the Indian social framework as she desires a dignified recognition of her individuality and respect for her multi-role contribution to the family. However, this desire remains a distant dream for most Indian women.

These questions always kept pondering me. During the past twenty-six years of my job, I have traveled extensively using all types of travel modes and classes. Hence, met women of all ages, all backgrounds, and all classes belonging to many religions and ethnic identities. During these travels, I always tried to interact with these women and understand the mindset they are into, enquiring about what goes into their minds and their perspectives in a given situation through informal conversations. This has enriched my knowledge and widened my understanding of common women. I found that problems, concerns, their thinking about themselves as women remained more or less the same across the country. Their value system and beliefs are largely governed by the ecosystem that surrounds them and the socio-cultural milieu plays a greater part in making these women an individual.

Somewhat the same experience Dr. Jaya also had in her professional life and travel experiences. So, when we met and had a heart-to-heart talk on this subject then we decided to club our experiences with the secondary information available through various sources and bring it as a book before the readers. The present book **"Indian Women: A Struggled Legacy and Reality"** is an attempt to provide some fresh perspective to the topic and hope it will be well taken by the prospective readers.

The book has been divided into fourteen comprehensive chapters covering almost all the dimensions related to the topic. These are –

Chapter one "Women in Early India" explains the status of women from the pre-Vedic period to the Later Vedic Period. How it changed and various phases this change went through. This also tries to analyze the reasons behind this change with ample evidence.

Chapter two "Role of Indian Women in Family & Society" discusses multiple roles, in general, the Indian women have to play.

Chapter three details current **"Traditional Customs for Women"** in Indian society. Traditional customs shave the greatest impact on all spheres of life of women in Indian society as they are deeply rooted and reflected in the attitudes of individuals. This shapes the mindset of individuals and women being weak suffers the most.

Family and Marriage in Indian socio-cultural structure are two institutions that are determinants of the status of women. How and to what extent is what that has been elaborated in **Chapter four- "Issues Related to Marriage and Family"**

Chapter five- "Missing Girl Child: The Female Foeticide-Violation of Right to life" discusses the brutal practice of killing a girl child fetus, its reasons, and implications at length.

There are various forms of domestic violence that Indian women face in their day to life and still remain silent most of the time. Indian Government has brought very strict laws against it yet this problem exists on a large scale. **Chapter six- "Domestic Violence Against Women: Many Facets"** talks in detail about this problem.

One of the most atrocious acts a male can do to a woman is an acid attack if his malevolent wish is not fulfilled. **Chapter seven - "Acid Attack on Women: A Cowardly Crime"** encounters the consequences a woman faces acid attack and the mentality that works behind it.

Chapter eight viz., **"Sexual Abuse Against Women: A Common Practice"** describes all forms of sexual abuse and their redressal mechanism.

"Women in Employment: Situation at Work Place" covers various types of abuse and inequalities a woman has to go through at their workplaces in **Chapter nine**

Chapter ten - "Dowry: Cause for Injustice from Womb to Tomb". This chapter gives a deep insight about Dowry system in India and their Laws.

Another major issue due to which women bear immense physical torture, social disrespect, and innumerable economic misery, is the problem of alcoholism by their spouses. Chapter eleven-**"Women and Alcoholism: Unending Agony and Anguish"** speaks suffering of women due to this particular problem and provides suggestions too. Interestingly the chapter also covers the other side of the coin which is the increasing trend of alcohol consumption by women in the current time and its adverse impact on their lives and health.

Mental health as a field of expertise, has recently, especially post-covid emerged as an extremely relevant part of the health of an individual. This crucial yet considered less important aspect till now is the topic of the next chapter. **Chapter twelve deals** with **"Women and Mental Illness: A Neglected Aspect."**

"Health Concerns of Women: Matter of Access and Outreach" is **Chapter thirteen** that discusses multiple health issues and related detrimental consequences women have to face. This also provides the answer to the problem.

Chapter fourteen, "Women and Migration: In Search of Better and Safe life" talks about the reasons for migration, and not only immediate atrocities but also long-term consequences women have to face as migrants.

Education: An Instrument for Empowerment (Chapter fifteen)enquires about how education can bring and lead to a far-reaching change in the lives of women

It is proven again and again that if women are given the right to raise their voices at a political platform with sufficient representation and make law for themselves in a democratic setup it may be the most effective affirmative action towards empowerment of women. **"Political Inclusion: Struggle for Power Sharing and Representation" (Chapter sixteen)** tries to delve into its reasons and solutions.

Nowadays women are coming out of four walls and shifting to big cities due to their jobs or in search of jobs to fulfill their dreams therefore a new challenge has arisen to provide them a safer and smooth life in their new ecosystem. **Chapter seventeen women's Safety in Cityscape: Securing Urban Spaces"** covers it all.

In today's world media has a daunting and everlasting impact on the minds of its receivers or viewers. This may make or tarnish images, may present a true picture, or manipulate situations and events through its multiple platforms. This has emerged as one of the most powerful players in today's geopolitical socio- culture scenario. **Chapter eighteen- Women and Media: The Darker Side** is an attempt towards reality check of portrayal and presentation of women in media.

Technology has appeared as a boon as well as a bane to society. Women being the soft target are getting caught in several types of cybercrimes and crimes against women in cyberspaces are on rising. **Chapter nineteen named"Women and Cyber Crime- Recent Threat from Technology"** covers this critical facet.

Chapter twenty- Rights of Women: The Legal Framework and Constitutional Provisionstries to delve into all affirmative actions taken and legal provisions made to tackle various oppressive activities and crimes against women by the Indian State.

We are very optimistic that this book would prove to be an extremely invaluable resource for all academicians, research scholars and senior researchers, faculty, and students of Humanities, Social Sciences, Women studies, and all other allied fields. We are expecting that policy planners, people working for the cause of women and their welfare, advocacy, and other social sector professionals would also be benefitted from this book. For us, it is a must-read for every woman.

Dr. Jaya Bharti and Dr. Hitaishi Singh

Acknowledgements

Writing a book on women being a woman was really hard for us but it was even more rewarding than that we had ever imagined. In the course of writing various chapters there were times that made us emotional, choked and found lack of words to express. There were times when we felt that we are reliving our lives. However, there were a number of people who remained our support system in many ways. They encouraged us, kept our spirits high and rendered their helping hand directly or indirectly. These handful people have been immense sources of constant inspiration and kept us going. Their critical reviews on the draft made this book better. Now it's our turn to extend our heartfelt thanks to all of them.

First and foremost, we are eternally grateful to the supreme almighty for showering His blessings on us and making this book possible.

We would like to extend our deepest gratitude to **Dr Rashmi Sinha, former State Director, Mahila Samakhya, Uttar Pradesh,** India,for her quick response to our request to write the foreword of our book and sparing her invaluable time for us.

The blessings showered and of our parents, in- laws are constant strength for us. They taught us discipline, mutual respect, empathy, dedication, hard work, honesty, gratitude and much more that has helped us in completing this and many other projects like this jointly.

This work would not have been a reality without the unconditional moral support and help of our families at every step - our brothers, sisters, and ever supportive kids Shuchita, Aparimita and the little new member of our family,Anvay.

We sincerely thank our better halves, Mr. Manoj Kumar Singh (Dr. Hitaishi Singh's husband) and Mr. Shivendra Pal (Dr. Jaya's husband) for their persistent support and constructive criticism, a necessary ingredient for any good piece of work.

The excellent team of our publishers of Notion Press needs special mention for their frequent feedback, hard work and dedication. Thank you once again for believing in us and considering the manuscript for publishing under your prestigious publication.

Last but not the least, we are truly grateful to all our teachers, friends, collogues and well-wishers who have been endless sourceof motivation.

Dr. Hitaishi Singh and Dr. Jaya Bharti

"Gender inequality, which remains pervasive worldwide, tends to lower the productivity of labor and the efficiency of labor allocation in households and the economy, intensifying the unequal distribution of resources. It also contributes to the non-monetary aspects of poverty – lack of security, opportunity and empowerment – that lower the quality of life for both men and women. While women and girls bear the largest and most direct costs of these inequalities, the costs cut broadly across society, ultimately hindering development and poverty reduction." – The Gender and Development Group -World Bank, from the report "Gender Equality and the Millennium Development Goals" (2003)

1
WOMEN IN EARLY INDIA

—❤—

During the ancient period of India, women played a significant role. The Rig Vedic Women in India enjoyed high status in society. Their condition was good. The women were provided an opportunity to attain high intellectual and spiritual standards. While the Vedic period (2000-500 BCE) is seen specifically as a 'Golden age' for women, there are also sweeping generalizations regarding the celebrated position of women during all of the ancient Indian period.

Position during the 'Golden Vedic age':

1. Goddesses were worshipped: There was no easy or automatic translation of goddess worship into actual changes for real women. The only thing that can be concluded from this is that divinity could be imagined in a feminine form by the people. We definitely cannot jump to the result that all women enjoyed political power and prestige just because we find evidence of goddess worship in this period.

2. Rig Veda has hymns composed by women and women sages existed: Out of over 1,000 hymns in the Rig Veda, only 12-15 are attributed to women. Clearly, this is not much cause for celebration. What this suggests is that women had limited access to sacred learning.

"Women must try to do things as men have tried. When they fail, their failure must be but a challenge to others."

3. Women also performed sacrifices: Women were allowed to perform sacrifices on behalf of their husbands, but never in their own right. A true marker of political privilege could be if they were the givers or receivers of dana or dakshina (booty from cattle raid). However, they don't appear to be in such roles.

In fact, for the later Vedic period during 800 BCE – 400 BCE, the historian Kumkum Roy argues how rituals conducted in the household were important to validate the control the male patriarch had over material resources and the reproductive role of women. Due to the emergence of the state (Rajya), the king assumed the role of the protector of the social order. He gained control over coercive power (danda), chariots, etc. This display of power inspired the ordinary householder to exercise control over women and the performance of rituals was one of the ways to achieve that. Women were therefore seen as property, either gifted away to priests or to others in marriage. Moreover, these popular and easily available views have 180 years of dialogue and discussions behind them. They have been strongly influenced, shaped, and informed by oppressive ideas disseminated by privileged men. They have a history and politics of their own, which shows that these are not given 'facts of history that we can accept uncritically.

In the context of Hinduism, the status of women was judged solely in legal and religious terms and studied mainly from religious texts of the Brahmanical tradition. Legal matters like the right to property, institutions of stridhana (gifts given to women before and after marriage) and niyoga (the practice of marrying off a widow to her brother-in-law), and religious affairs like a performance of sacrifices became important in the debates around status of women.

These Brahmanical texts, used by the religious reformers and even their opponents, were compiled and transmitted by Brahmins. Therefore, these texts carried their inherent bias, were unreflective of realities of ordinary people, and restricted to upper castes – what they provided was only an incomplete view from the standpoint of privileged men.

Hence, our current obsession to celebrate the respectable position of women based on their role in family and marriage goes back to the 19th-century nationalist struggle. Not only are this criterion of progress flimsy and selective but also extremely simplistic. These are ideas based on unreliable sources which were churned out by upper-caste men belonging to the middle-class section of society. Hinduism in its Sanskritic form was seen as the essential culture of India. This is seen in how the Gupta period because it experienced a high volume of the production of Sanskrit literature, was seen as the 'Golden period' of 'Hindu' India as it was believed that during this time Hinduism became popular again. Other cultures were seen as intrusions and very often the coming of Muslims in India was held responsible for problems plaguing the Indian society.

Hinduism in its Sanskritic form was seen as the essential culture of India. This is seen in how the Gupta period because it experienced a high volume of the production of Sanskrit literature, was seen as the 'Golden period' of 'Hindu' India as it was believed that during this time Hinduism became popular again. Other cultures were seen as intrusions and very often the coming of Muslims in India was held responsible for problems plaguing the Indian society.

In the ancient Indus valley, the civilization of India, evidence shows the worship of the mother goddess. Hence, the veneration for the mother is evident during that period. During the Rig Vedic period, it is believed that the position of wife was honored and women's position was acknowledged, especially in the performance of religious ceremonies. The education of young girls was considered an important qualification for marriage. There are references in Vedic literature that in the Kshatriya society, brides had the exclusive right of selecting their own consorts, which was known as 'Swayamvara'. In Rig Vedic society, the dowry system was unknown. However, the concept of marriage as dan or gift was prevalent. Monogamy was the general practice though Bigamy was also in practice, it was limited to the aristocratic classes. The wife was respected in her new house. The wife participated in the sacrificial offerings of her husband.

Pre-Vedic Period:

The recorded history of India began with the arrival of Aryans in the 15th Century B.C. When Vedic Era began, the patriarchal culture has eliminated the matriarchal culture. It could be considered the beginning of gender discrimination in India. The historical period marked by Rigveda reveals the predominance of religious concern over civil life. Vedic culture was widespread until the arrival of the Muslims in the 8th Century. The period that followed the Muslim invasion is considered medieval history in India which also witnessed the predominance of patriarchal culture. With regard to the patriarchal ordering of social life, the Islamic era did not differ much from that of the Vedic era. What followed the Muslim era is the British Raj in the 18th Century. It was also predominantly patriarchal. Throughout the past centuries, the patriarchy and the patriarchal social organization prevailed – so too the gender discrimination. A survey of Vedas, Puranas, Upanishads, and Epics reveals the status of women and their struggle for power in ancient India. The status of women during the pre-Vedic period is not clear. It is believed that prehistoric man who lived in the Paleolithic age was a nomad. Food gathering was the chief occupation. Culture and civilization are the attributes of Neolithic man who became a food producer leaving slowly the style of food gathering. Men began to settle down on river valleys. Indus valley civilization which was the first known civilization in India is said to have flourished in the 25th Century B.C.

Women in Vedic Literature

The Vedic period witnessed the historical development of human civilization from nomadic style to settled style. During the early Vedic era, there is evidence to show that woman was given some respect and opportunities in domestic life. She was considered the creator, protector, and educator of her children. Women were given opportunities to offer sacrifices along with their husbands. A man could not become a spiritual whole unless he was accompanied by his wife. The gods were thought not to accept the materials offered by a bachelor. Sati did not exist in this period. Widowed mothers were protected by their sons. Rigveda the first Vedic script brings to light the culture and civilization of early invaders to India who was predominantly nomadic. The society had not yet settled down with farming. They were mainly food gatherers. Society in the Rig-Vedic period was prominently pastoral and it did not produce a surplus to allow any section to be completely subordinated or withdrawn from the process of production. Both the men and women were engaged in food gathering and partook equally in the struggle for survival. Each family was a single economic unit without any specialization or gender-based division of labor. Both men and women could participate equally in all the political, economic, and religious affairs, which were very simple in terms of organization and functioning. This perhaps explains the comparatively better situation of women in the Vedic period in terms of access to education, religious rights, freedom of movement, etc.

Women during Later Vedic Age

Ramayana and Mahabharata are the great epics of India. The lifestyle presented in these epics reflects the contemporary socio-economic reality. Mahabharata, which is written presumably later, presents a story prior to that of Ramayana. The social life presented by Ramayana and Mahabharata may be the first written record of the Hindu way of living. The popular form of marriage as seen in the epics is Swayamvara. Swayamvara is the institution of marriage, especially among the higher castes. In this ancient form of marriage, women were said to have exercised the freedom and autonomy to select their life partners. Sita of Ramayana and Draupadi of Mahabharat married by way of Swayamvara. Swayamvara does not give the freedom of choice to the bride in the modern sense, because often her freedom to choose her husband is limited. In the institution of 'Swayamvara', she is compelled to marry the winner of a competition, conducted to prove the martial excellence of her prospective bridegrooms.

There was gradual degeneration in the status of women in India after the Vedic age. The caste system and ritualism began to take deep root in the lives of the common man. Child marriage and Sati became popular. Buddhism and Jainism emerged as alternative religious orders devoid of caste-based social order. These new religions professed equality between men and women but had little impact on rural masses. Among the intellectuals, they appeared as strong countercurrents for caste-ridden Hindu society. Till the arrival of the Muslims, Hindu philosophy was the guiding force for the masses in India. Patriarchal social order backed with religious sanctions nurtured gender discrimination in the economic, political, and social life of traditional communities in India. Education of women, which was an accepted norm during the Vedic period, slowly began to be neglected, and later on, girls were totally denied any access to education.

Every human society is invariably characterized by social differentiations. Gender-based differentiation is one. Men had the role of earning and women had the role of reproduction of heirs and homemaking. A historical understanding of the status of women in early Indian society shows a declining trend in the position of women. The historical analysis of the position of women in ancient India shows that women did not share an equal position with men.

The Rig Vedic period produced women seers who were the products of cultivated disciplines and contributed in the writing of Vedas. In that simplistic society, women took an active part in agriculture, in manufacturing bows and arrows, and, in weaving cloth. By and large, monogamy was the rule. Re-marriage of widows was permitted. The position of the wife was an honored one in the family.

Even in post- Rig Vedic, Puranic and Buddhist times women were not the chattels that they became in the dark medieval ages. They enjoyed a fair amount of personal freedom. They were the equals of men in their rights and privileges in society. They had access to education, high learning, and training as well as participation in all functions.

In the 18th century, the British tried to effect certain modifications in the Indian social structure. Laws were passed to permit inter-caste marriages, widow re-marriage, and divorce under certain conditions, always careful not to hurt conservative susceptibilities. Facilities were provided for the education of women. These moves brought about an awareness of the prevalent wrongs in the system and a quest for the revival of old values and

social patterns.

❦❦❦

2

ROLE OF INDIAN WOMEN IN FAMILY & SOCIETY

In the decade ahead, Indian women appear to be determined to devote individual and collective attention to the problems irking them and launch a cleansing crusade in the thinking patterns of society, educate public opinion at all levels to sweep aside anachronistic values, and discard the dead and decadent elements in Indian culture and rebuild the vitally, progressive ones.

-Asha Dhar

Women are and have always been actors and agents in history along with men, as also an equal participants in the process of evolution and fruition of any civilization. Since women are half and sometimes more than half of humankind, they always have shared the world stage and its activities equally with men. As such, women have always been central, not marginal, to the making of society and to the building of civilization. Women have also shared with men in preserving collective memory, which shapes the past into cultural tradition, provides the link between generations, and connects the present with the past and the future.

The woman performs the role of wife, partner, organizer, administrator, director, re-creator, disburser, economist, mother, disciplinarian, teacher, health officer, artist, and queen in the family at the same time. Apart from it, a woman plays a key role in the socio-economic development of society. Modern education and modern economic life use to compel women more and more to leave the narrow sphere of the family circle and work side by side for the enrichment of society. She can be a member of any women's organization and can launch various programs like literacy programs such as adult education, education for disadvantaged girls, etc. Women are the key to sustainable development and quality of life. So they should be members of community centers or clubs to disseminate knowledge about handicraft, cottage industries, food preservation, and low-cost nutritious diet to people belonging to low socio-economic status for their economic upliftment. They should act as leaders of the society to raise voices against women's violence, exploitation in a household as well as in the workplace, dowry prohibition superstition, and other social atrocities.

However, notwithstanding the cardinal role of women in the process of the evolution and development of human civilization, it is ironic that historical scholarship has mostly seen the depiction and portrayal of women as marginal to the making of civilization. There exists a contradiction between women's centrality and active role in creating a society and they're perceived and highlighted marginality, emphasized on the basis of an ill-founded claim of knowing their history and thus being well equipped to interpret and evaluate it. Historical scholarship, up to the most recent past, has seen women as marginal to the making of civilization and as unessential to those pursuits defined as having historic significance. Thus the recorded and interpreted record of the past of the human race is only a partial record, in that it omits the past of half of humankind, and it is distorted, in that it tells the story from the viewpoint of the male half of humanity only. No man has been excluded from the historical record because of his sex, yet all women were.

A disparity in the social role of men and women and the lack of parity in their respective positions in society are noticeable among virtually all cultures and societies in the world, even if the degree and level of such inequality vary from one society to another. From the perspective of an ideal situation for the smooth working of social order, the society may be compared to a bird whose two wings represent men and women, entailing an arrangement in the context of the social order where the two sexes command an even and balanced position. Unfortunately, the society's two wings, constituting men and women, are very unbalanced and ill-proportioned in India, when it comes to their social role and their status and position in society. Such disparity between the position of men and women in the Indian society raises the 'woman question', which, however, cannot be satisfactorily understood by referring to the aspects and the factors related to women alone. In fact, it is obvious that such social disparity is rooted in the ideological environment and the overall social and cultural setting of a particular social system, which are expressed through its characteristic social customs and institutions. These customs and institutions affect women directly, often imposing limitations and restrictions upon their rights and freedom and playing a decisive role in determining the overall position of women in society. Hence, for a proper understanding of the women's position and status in a society, it is imperative to critically examine how these customs and institutions evolve, and how the society's ideological milieu makes them function in a particular way, generally for serving the interest of the patriarchy.

In general, men hold power in all the important institutions of a patriarchal society; this however does not imply that women are totally powerless or totally without rights, influence, and resources under patriarchy. In fact, no unequal system can continue without the participation of the oppressed, some of whom derive some benefits from it. This is true of patriarchies as well. Women have risen to power, been in control, have wrested benefits in greater or smaller measure. But all this does not change the fact that the system is male-dominated - women are merely accommodated in it in a variety of ways.

In India, patriarchy has been a system of benevolent paternalism in which obedient women were accorded certain rights, privileges, and security. This paternalism simultaneously made the insubordination invisible and led to their complicity in it. While the women participated in the process of their own subordination because they were psychologically shaped so as to internalize the idea of their own inferiority as they did elsewhere, in India they were also socialized into believing in their own empowerment through chastity and fidelity; through sacrifice, they saw themselves as achieving both sublimation and strength. Thus, they created strength out of their inferiority and weaknesses; through rich and imaginative mythology, women were spurred and prodded into accepting the ideology that genuine power lies in women's ability to sacrifice, in gaining spiritual strength by denying themselves access to power, or the means to it. Through the reiteration of cultural models in the mythology, women believed that they had different and distinctive power, a higher and more spiritual power, a power that would save their husbands from the worst fate and even absolve them of their sins and every woman in a subordinate one. Linked to this system is the ideology that men are superior to women, that women are and should be controlled by men and that women are part of men's property. In some South Asian languages, for example, the words used for a husband are swarni, shauhar, pati, malik - all words which mean "lord" or "owner". The nature of patriarchy varies and is different in different classes in the same society; in different societies, and in different periods in history. For example, the experience of patriarchy is different for tribal women and for upper-caste Hindu women; for women in the USA and women in India. Each social system or historical period has its own variations on how patriarchy functions, and how social and cultural practices differ. However, the broad principles remain the same, i.e. men are in control, although the nature of his control may differ.

In this context, it is pertinent to note Manu's observation on the subservience of women -

"Pita raksati kaumare bharta raksati yauvane...........Raksanti sthavireputra na strisvatantryamarhati"

"Her father protects (her) in childhood, her husband protects (her) in youth, and her sons protect (her) in old age, a woman is never fit for independence." Manu Dharmasastra thus clearly suggests that a woman should never be independent; as a daughter, she is under the surveillance of her father, as a wife of her husband, and as a widow of her son. Such disparaging characterization of women strengthens the idea of perpetual tutelage of Indian women. The Hindu sacred law prescribed and idealized that subordination. The society thus gradually established itself as patriarchal, controlling every aspect of women's existence.

COMMON ROLES OF WOMEN

- A Daughter: When she is born, she brings a new meaning to her parent's life. Many aspirations and dreams make way when the daughter is born in a family. It is quite a popular belief that a daughter cares for her folks more than a son would do. And it is true to an extent. Women are more sensitive and considerate, especially when it comes to bonds and relationships.
- A Sister: As a sister, a woman gives love and warmth to her brothers and sisters. It goes without saying that certain values and morals are not inherited or adapted, they are inborn traits those come as part and parcel of being a woman. To have a sister, who acts as a friend and a confidant too, is such a delight for any brother.
- A Friend: It is a scientifically proven fact that a female's body is equipped with hormones that make her more sensitive and emotional, than a man. This is what makes a woman a better friend. The ability to relate and analyze a situation compassionately makes it easier to resolve life, especially when it comes to friends.

- A Wife: When a man brings home a bride, he is always expecting that he has got a partner for life who is going to make his life happy and joyful. Often, in doing so, many times her own dreams get sacrificed, but that goes without a complaint.
- A Daughter In Law: With married life, comes a new role. To be the daughter of a new set of parents. And she takes this one up with the equaled love and compassion. She goes a step ahead and accepts them as her own parents and showers devotion to them; takes care of them in old age and fulfills the voids in their lives.
- A Mother: When she becomes a mother, she takes a new birth in the form of her own children. Because she starts seeing a new life right from the beginning. She becomes the mentor, the friend, the philosopher, and the guide too.
- A Professional: In today's times, when education is imperative and a career for a woman is no more a taboo, women are pronouncing their presence in the professional world with enhanced power and enthusiasm. Entrepreneurs, businesswomen, CEOs, and high profile professionals, we have a fleet of them around us.
- A Mother In Law: Then comes a time when she weds off her prized possessions, her children, and becomes a mother-in-law, welcoming new additions to the family and promising them home just like the one they bid farewell to.
- A Grandmother: As she ages, she takes up a new role of becoming a grandparent to the newest of the family, her grandchildren. Moments spent huddled close to our grandma, listening to her stories, while eating the delicious goodies she prepares for us, stays etched in our minds forever.
- A caregiver: Now this is a role that starts right from the time she is conscious of the world's happenings. First, she cares for her family, parents, and friends, then she cares for her partner and his/her family, then she moves a step higher and learns to care for her own child, and so on. By the end of her life, a woman has managed to carefully make space for so many people in her life. She knows exactly what everyone needs and wants and makes

sure that this is fulfilled by either working for it herself or giving others the environment to work for it.

- A primary educator: A woman, more importantly, a mother is a primary educator of her house. A child learns their first habits and doings from their mothers, in fact right from the time they are in the womb. She carries the responsibility of creating good human beings who will prove to be responsible citizens in the future. Not just for the child, but a woman can be a role model for everyone around her, and how she conducts herself has the ability to influence others.

- A friend: Probably one of the most underrated roles of a woman. It is scientifically proven that women are more emotional and understanding towards other people in comparison to men, hence women are actually better friends than they are perceived to be. A woman is a friend who listens, empathizes, and gives advice when necessary. The caregiver in her takes a front role for her friends as well.

- A changemaker: For centuries women have been the front runners when it comes to making changes in the house and the society, be it something as big as fighting for equal rights to votes or something as small as deciding what her family will eat so as to remain healthy. A woman has the ability to bring about a change by voicing her opinions where necessary. Women have fought for everything they deserve and today we are at a position where we can say that we are almost at par with men. Of course, some changes still need to be made, but I can confidently say that this will also be led by women.

- A professional: This is one of the only roles in which she does everything selfishly, and rightly so. Her desire to succeed in her career and make a name for herself is something she chooses to do for her satisfaction and happiness. It is also one of the most challenging roles because women are expected to hone the skill of acing this role, without compromising on any of the above-mentioned roles. Today women are an active part of the work environment in every field be it business, service, entertainment, or even agriculture.

Don't go through life, grow through life.-Eric Butterworth

It is during the last few decades that women and their organizations have been challenging patriarchy in different ways. In a way, women's conceptualization of patriarchy, their attempts to analyze it as a system and to deconstruct it are in themselves a powerful challenge. The subsequent application of this analysis to action at several levels - academic, grassroots, regional and international, and in society in general- has placed the issue of women's subordination on most national agendas. It is however a very recent phenomenon that even women have started writing from the perspective of the woman.

In the wake of Raja Ram Mohan Roy's movement against women's subjugation to men and British influence on Indian culture and civilization, the position of women had once again undergone a change. However, it was only under the enlightened leadership of Mahatma Gandhi that they re-asserted their equality with men. In response to the call of Gandhi they discarded their veil and came out of the four walls of their houses to fight the battle of freedom shoulder to shoulder with their brothers. The result is that the Indian Constitution today has given to women the equal status with men. There is no discrimination between men and women. All professions are open to both of them with merit as the only criterion of selection.

As a result of their newly gained freedom Indian woman have distinguished themselves in various spheres of life as politicians, orators, lawyers, doctors, administrators and diplomats. They are not only entrusted with work of responsibility but also they perform their duties very honestly and sincerely. There is hardly any sphere of life in which Indian women have not taken part and shown their worth. Women exercise their right to vote, contest for Parliament and Assembly, seek appointment in public office and compete in other spheres of life with men. This shows that women in India enjoy today more liberty and equality than before. They have acquired more liberty to participate in the affairs of the country. They have been given equality with men in shaping their future and sharing responsibilities for themselves, their family and their country.

Out of the several factors that justify the greatness of India's ancient culture, one of the greatest, is the honored place ascribed to women. Manu, the great law-giver, said long ago, 'where women are honored there reside the gods'. According to ancient Hindu scriptures, no religious rite can be performed with perfection by a man without the participation of his wife. The wife's participation was made and still continued to be essential to any religious rite. Married men were allowed to perform sacred rites along with their wives on the occasion of various important festivals. Wives are thus befittingly called 'Ardhangani' (better half). They are given not only important but equal positions with men. But in the later period, the position of women went on deteriorating due to Muslim influence. During the Muslim period of history, they were deprived of their rights of equality with men. In tune with the global phenomenon, educated and modern Indian women seem

to have formed a vision of equality with men. They have acquired a tremendous zeal to secure what they call 'lost rights.' Blatantly, they appear bent on ensuring their individuality to gain the freedom to explore their potential as integrated human beings. They no longer consider themselves silent spectators in this dynamic world situation but feel an urgent obligation to action and role-contribution. They urge breaking away from hackneyed traditions, warped social thinking, and double standards of morality, that have blocked the worthwhile contributions they could make to the country's welfare.

There is no denying the fact that women in India have made a considerable progress in the last fifty years but yet they have to struggle against many handicaps and social evils in the male dominated society. The Hindu Code Bill has given the daughter and the son equal share of the property. The Marriage Act no longer regards woman as the property of man. Marriage is now considered to be a personal affair and if a partner feels dissatisfied she or he has the right of divorce. But passing of law is one thing and its absorption in the collective thinking of society is quite a different matter. In order to prove themselves equal to the dignity and status given to them in the Indian Constitution they have to shake off the shackles of slavery and superstitions. They should help the government and the society in eradicating the evils of dowry, illiteracy and ignorance among the eves. The dowry problem has assumed a dangerous form in this country. The parents of the girls have to pay thousands and lacs to the bridegrooms and their greedy fathers and mothers. If promised articles are not given by the parents of brides, the cruel and greedy members of the bridegrooms' family take recourse to afflicting tortures on the married women. Some women are murdered in such cases. The dowry deaths are really heinous and barbarous crimes committed by the cruel and inhumane persons. The young girls should be bold enough in not marrying the boys who demand dowry through their parents. The boys should also refuse to marry if their parents demand dowry. But unfortunately the number of such bold and conscientious boys is very few. Even the doctors, engineers, teachers and the administrative officers do not hesitate in allowing themselves to be sold to the wealthy fathers of shy and timid girls. Such persons have really brought disgrace to their cadres in particular and society in general. The government should enact stringent laws to afflict rigorous punishment on dowry seekers, women's murderers and rapers.

3

TRADITIONAL CUSTOMS FOR WOMEN'S

It is never too late to give up your prejudices.
Henry David Thoreau

Walden

A family's honor is closely tied to the honor of their women, as reflected in the virginity of unmarried girls and the fidelity of married ones. Any hint of scandal can bring shame to an extended (joint) family, which can have dozens of members. This explains in part why a woman's actions and movements are so closely monitored. A man who is brazen enough to kiss a young girl in a field can get the shit kicked out of him and or even sometimes be killed. Rural women who deviate from the strict social codes are sometimes stripped naked in public or even gang-raped. Hindu women are expected to be shy and demure and not to speak unless they are spoken to. Indian women have traditionally kept their voices low, looked downward when speaking, and never looked a man in the eye. Men look down on women smokers even though men smoke everywhere and sometimes snub their cigarettes out on the floors of people's homes.

All moral codes say that women are to be treated with respect and kindness, mothers, particularly so. In many homes, there are separate areas for men and women. Sometimes men and women drive in separate cars. In cases of adultery, the man is often let off lightly and regarded only to take a ritualized purifying bath while the woman is regarded as polluted for the rest of her life. Other punishments might be imposed depending on the caste of the man and woman involved. One woman told National Geographic, "As a child, I was very fond of dancing but when I told my mother, she slapped me and said, 'Don't even think of it; girls from descent families don't dance and sing. Don't ever speak to me about it again."

Married women in India often have a dot between their eyes or at the parting of their hair. A widow is not supposed to have such a dot. Only married women, or in some cases women or girls who have never been married, can wear it. These many women wear dots of various colors, shapes, and sizes. They are worn for fashion, not religious reasons and often are designed to match the clothes they are wearing

In southern India, girls choose to wear a mark on their forehead, while in other parts of India it is the prerogative of the married woman. According to hinduism.about.com: "A red dot on the forehead is an auspicious sign of marriage and guarantees the social status and sanctity of the institution of marriage. The Indian bride steps over the threshold of her husband's home, bedecked in glittering apparels and ornaments, dazzling the red bindi on her forehead that is believed to usher in prosperity, and grants her a place as the guardian of the family's welfare and progeny." [Source: hinduism.about.com]

"A traditional bindi is red or maroon in color. A pinch of vermilion powder applied skillfully with a practiced fingertip makes the perfect red dot. Women who are not nimble-fingered take great pains to get the perfect round. They use small circular discs or hollow pie coins as an aid. First, they apply a sticky wax paste on the empty space in the disc. This is then covered with

kumkum or vermilion and then the disc is removed to get a perfect round bindi. Sandal, 'aguru', 'kasturi', 'kumkum' (made of red turmeric), and 'sindoor' (made of zinc oxide and dye) make this special red dot. Saffron ground together with 'kusumba' flower can also create the magic!"

Millions of Hindu and Muslim women in northern and central India, particularly in rural areas, practice "purdah", complex set rules for veiling and excluding women that some say have been followed for over 1000 years. Women according to purdah may not be seen by any men other than her husband and in some cases some of his in-laws. She may not even talk to her husband in public when other people are around; notes have to be given to children acting as messengers. [Source: Doranne Wilson Jacobson, National Geographic August 1977].

Many persons have a wrong idea of what constitutes true happiness. It is not attained through self-gratification, but through fidelity to a worthy purpose. -Helen Keller

Purdah rules of veiling the body and avoidance of public appearance, especially in the presence of relatives linked by marriage and before strange men, are inextricably linked to patterns of authority and harmony within the family. Rules of Hindu and Muslim purdah differ in certain key ways, but female modesty and decorum as well as concepts of family honor are essential to the various forms of purdah. In most areas, purdah restrictions are stronger for women of high-status families. The importance of purdah is not limited to family life; rather, these practices all involve restrictions on female activity and access to power and the control of vital resources in a male-dominated society. Restriction and restraint for women in virtually every aspect of life are the basic essentials of purdah. In India, both males and females are circumscribed in their actions by economic disabilities, hierarchical rules of deference in kinship groups, castes, and the larger society. But for women who observe purdah, there are additional constraints. Purdah is derived from the Hindi word "parda," literally meaning "curtain." It implies high status. Brahmans favor strict interpretations of the purdah dictums. Some old-timers lament how things have changed: how some young brides, who are supposed to be sequestered, are even talking to their father-in-laws. Hindu rules enforcing feminine modesty became stricter after the Muslim invasions so that Hindus could protect their women from the conquerors. Some scholars believe the custom of purdah was introduced by Muslims. There is little evidence of it existing before the arrival of large numbers of Muslims in the 12th century. Others have suggested that Hindus introduced the custom to Muslims.

1. During their lifetime some India women see nothing beyond their parent's and their husband's houses and few streets around these houses. Going to the well and attending religious functions are some of the few times women actually leave their house. They stay busy within their homes cooking, tending courtyard gardens and raising children. Some women are so deep in

purdah that when male guests come to their house they pass dinner through a curtained doorway.

2. Restricting women to household endeavors rather than involving them in tasks in fields and markets is associated with prestige and high rank in northern India. There the wealthiest families employ servants to carry water from the well and to work in the fields alongside family males. Mature women of these families may make rare appearances in the fields to bring lunch to the family males working there and sometimes to supervise laborers. Thus elitism is expressed in women's exclusive domesticity, with men providing economic necessities for the family. Only women of poor and low-ranking groups engage in heavy manual labor outside the home, especially for pay. Such women work long hours in the fields, on construction gangs, and at many other tasks, often veiling their faces as they work. [Source: Library of Congress *]

3. In rural communities and in older sections of cities, purdah observances remain vital, although they are gradually diminishing in intensity. Among the educated urban and rural elite, purdah practices are rapidly vanishing and for many have all but disappeared. Chastity and female modesty are still highly valued, but, for the elite, face-veiling and the burka are considered unsophisticated. As girls and women become more widely and more highly educated, female employment outside the home is commonplace, even for women of elite families.

In the Vedic age and even in the post-Vedic era, we don't find any veil custom. The veil isn't mentioned in Arthashastra, Manumsriti..... Neither smritis nor any Purans mentioned any such thing. Also, Indic religions like [(Hindu, Budh, Sikh, Jain) isms} never sanctioned any veil. This means that it is more a social issue...However, around same time we have some words in Sanskrit;

· **avagunthana meaning cloak-veil,**

- uttariya meaning shoulder-veil,
- adhikantha pata meaning neck-veil, and
- sirovas-tra meaning head-veil

To most Westerners, veiling is more associated with Muslims than Hindus. There is some debate as to when the custom of veiling began and where the custom originated. Some conservative Muslims have insisted that veiling was practiced in Mohammed's time and Mohammed's wives veiled themselves. There is little evidence of this though. Some say the custom of veiling was adopted by Muslims about three of four generations after Mohammed's death and is believed to have been copied from the Byzantines or perhaps from India or Persia. Veiling has also been practiced for a long time by Hindus from India, where women seclude and veil themselves through a custom called purdah, which was originally adopted by the upper classes and became a status symbol. In any case, the custom of veiling predates Islam. In antiquity, it was a sign of high status. Jewish and Christian women adopted the custom to symbolize a retreat from public life. The Iranian term chador, meaning "tent." is derived from the personal custom of very wealthy women traveling around in covered sedan chairs. Some people have said the Western custom of brides wearing veils comes from Muslim countries. More likely it comes from ancient Greece. The veiling and segregation of women was common practice among women in ancient Greece, Rome, and Byzantium. In the old days veiling was more common in the cities than in villages, presumably because city women were more likely to be secluded and pampered than rural women who needed to work in the fields, and veiling and covering themselves made such work more difficult. In the cities, it seems that women often were the ones that demanded they be veiled as a means of escaping harassment and showing their status.

Many of feminine modesty are not considered purdah but merely proper female behavior. For traditional Hindus of northern and central India, purdah observances begin at marriage, when a woman acquires a husband and in-laws. Although she almost never observes purdah in her natal home or before her natal relatives, a woman does observe purdah in her husband's home and before his relatives. As a young woman, she remains inside her husband's house much of the time (rather than going out into lanes or fields), absents herself or covers her face with her sari in the presence of senior males and females related by marriage, and, when she does leave the house in her marital village, covers her face with her sari. Such practices help shield women from unwanted male advances and control women's sexuality but also express relations within and between groups of kin. Familial prestige, household harmony, social distance, affinal respect, property ownership, and local political power are all linked to purdah. [Source: Library of Congress. Through use of the end of the sari as a face veil and deference of manner, a married woman shows respect to her affinal kin who are older than or equal to her husband in age, as well as certain other relatives. She may speak to the women before whom she veils, but she usually does not converse with the men. Exceptions to this are her husband's younger brothers, before whom she may veil her face, but with whom she has a warm joking relationship involving verbal banter. Initially almost faceless and voiceless in her marital home, a married woman matures and gradually relaxes some of these practices, especially as elder in-laws become senescent or die and she herself assumes senior status. In fact, after some years, a wife may neglect to veil her face in front of her husband when others are present and may even speak to her husband in public. For Muslim women, purdah practices involve less emphasis on veiling from in-laws and more emphasis on protecting women from contact with strangers outside the sphere of kinship. Because Muslims often marry cousins, a woman's in-laws may also be her natal relatives, so veiling her face within the marital home is often inappropriate. Unlike Hindus, Muslim women do not veil from other women as do Hindus. Traditional Muslim women and even unmarried girls, however, often refrain from appearing in public, or if they do go out, they wear an all-covering garment known as a burka , with a full face covering. A burka protects a woman — and her family — from undue familiarity with unknown outsiders, thus emphasizing the unity of the family vis-à-vis the outside world. Because Muslim women are entitled to a share in the family real estate, controlling their relationships with males outside the family can be crucial to the maintenance of family property and prestige.

4

ISSUES FACED BY WORKING MARRIED WOMEN

❦

There can be hope only for a society
which acts as one big family,
not as many separate ones.

<u>Anwar Sadat</u>

Marriage traditionally has become virtually essential for every woman; therefore, lone women are not much-accepted form in Indian society. Consequently, they are more or less subject to insolence in society. Among lone women, divorced or separated women are the most unwanted sect in the society because according to Hindu ideology, marriage is a sacred relationship that is in vogue for procreation and continuation of family lineage only. It cannot be dissolved through a divorce or any other means on personal grounds. However, the Hindu civil code permits divorce in modern India, still it is not gladly accepted in society. During the neoliberal period, Indian society, culture, and economy are more or less dominated by the market. Marriage in this background does not lose its traditional significance; rather, patriarchy has transformed marriage into a market-friendly way. Still now, the conception of parents regarding settlement of their offsprings includes both economic as well as marital settlement.

You must work – we must all work – to make the world worthy of its children.-Pablo Casals

Following Indian culture, parents, therefore, feel their responsibility to arrange a marriage for their offspring, particularly for their daughters so that they can live with dignity. In this society, women's dignity, respect, empowerment are steered by their marital status. Serving in-laws are recognized as an important function of women because patriarchy expects subordination of women. Reproduction has always been considered an important part of Indian women's life and is prioritized overproduction. Marriage, therefore, becomes the only option for future settlement of Indian women in absence of their parents since it takes care of their security and livelihood. In such a social environment, women's decision to remain single (unmarried, separated, and divorcee) is codified as denial to their assigned duty of reproduction and transmitting the traditional social rules and values across generations. Moreover, there is a possibility of facing social and economic insecurity in absence of adequate income. Based on the above discussion, it can be argued that the entire life of Indian women is regulated by their marital status. Even, their status in the family and society depends on their marital status. Most of the time lone women get lower status in society and are subject to disrespect as well as physical and mental abuse.

Success can become an obstacle in marriage for a woman and when it is not accomplished according to her unrealistic expectations, the progress can seem slow and begin to shake the root of her relationship with her man. When you allow your friend's marriage to define your own success, you will be disappointed to know that the grass is not greener elsewhere. Choose to challenge your delusion and redefine your understanding of marital success and learn to love and appreciate what your man brings to the table. After all, it takes a woman to bring out the best in her life partner.

Every woman faces hardship in her married life. It's a given. In the history of human development, women have been as vital in history-making as men have been. In fact, higher status for women vis-à-vis employment and work performed by them in a society is a significant indicator of a nation's overall progress. Undoubtedly, without the active participation of women in national activities, the social, economic, or political progress of a country will deteriorate and become stagnant. But ironically and tragically, women employees in general, are not taken very seriously by their superiors, colleagues, or society at large. Having a career poses challenges for women due to their family responsibilities. Traditionally Indian women had been homemakers but in recent decades, proper education and better awareness, in addition to the ever-increasing cost of living have made them go out and choose careers. In a patriarchal society like India, it is still believed that a man is the primary breadwinner of his family. Although Indian women have started working outside their homes still they have a long way to go both culturally, socially, and economically, to bring in positive attitudinal changes in the mindset of people. It is generally perceived that gender bias against working women starts right from the stage of recruitment. Most of the Indian men are not ready to accept that women are capable enough to work side by side with men in all the sectors, other than in a few limited ones like teaching, nursing, and clerical sectors. Their capabilities are generally underestimated as a result of which Indian women have a tendency to opt for less demanding jobs even if they are highly qualified. Women have the responsibility to effectively manage their multiple roles in domestic as well as professional lives. Men generally do not offer any help in the households work. This makes the life of working women extremely stressful.

While a majority of married women still face discrimination and gender bias, in the last few decades, the number of women successful in politics, technology and business, etc. is definitely on the rise. Society has started seeing women from a different perspective. They work as lawyers, nurses, doctors, social workers, teachers, secretaries, managers, officers, etc. There is no profession today where women are not employed. However, it is true that working women have to face problems by virtue of their sex. For centuries women have been subjected to exploitation and torture, physically, sexually, and mentally. There are innumerable challenges and problems faced by them both at home and workplace. What we generally see today, in addition to various media and journal reports is that in the workplace women generally face mental stress, sexual harassment, discriminatory practices, safety and security issues, etc (Martin, 1989). India's patriarchal society thinks of women only as homemakers and sexual objects and is generally subjected to exploitation and torture (Dube, 2001).

To be precise, here are some of the common challenges faced by working women along with a few ways and means to overcome them.

1. Inability to maintain a work-life balance – For a mother, working full-time can be extremely tedious and exhausting. Besides having to handle their professional work, they also have to tend to their household chores and look after their kid. This drastically affects their work-life balance and takes a toll on their emotional as well as mental health.

2. Constant grapple with guilt – Mothers are truly one of a kind. While as an individual, they have dreams and aspirations,

according to the societal norms, like mothers, they must also be the sole nurturers in the family. This is why there is a constant and ceaseless feeling of guilt that remains in the conscience of all mothers, where if they choose their careers over their home, they are placed in a questionable position.

3. A rift between passion and obligation – Daring to dream and being ambitious are two aspects of human nature. But considering a working mother must also tend to the needs of her family, there is always an underlying conflict between what she wants and what she must do.

4. Priorities are questioned – There is a great disparity between how we look at working men and working women. While men have always worked in the public domain, their sense of responsibility towards their family is limited to the role of a breadwinner as opposed to the role of women as house-makers. Therefore, once women step into the professional world their sense of commitment towards their families is often questioned and their priorities need to be set right away.

5. Never-ending efforts to multitask – Another common challenge faced by working women is the constant need to multitask. Whether they are working at the office or from home, they must constantly tackle their time between their personal and professional life.

6. No time for 'Self'- A working woman, while performing the role of the mother and a professional, forgets to invest any time in herself. There is no recreation period for them, even when they are on work leave. It's either this or that. There is just no time for oneself.

7. The need to be perfect all the time – Well, surely working women are the modern-day representation of a superwoman, however, they cannot be perfect all the time. The societal expectations and the need to be perfect all the time can sometimes take a great toll on mothers, especially the ones who are also working.

While it may seem extremely difficult to break away from the troubles of being a working mother as well as a full-time mother, there is always a solution to tackle these situations in life. That being said, if you're a working mom and are facing similar challenges, here are a few ways you can overcome them with just some extra effort.

1. -Organize and plan your work for the day beforehand so that you can manage your time efficiently.
2. Make sure to develop a relationship, where your partner or your husband acknowledges his role as a parent too and puts in the same effort you do in taking care of the family.
3. Maintain cordial relationships with your relatives and siblings so that you can approach them easily in times of an emergency.
4. Make sure that your colleagues and superiors know the importance of your child and your family so in times of urgency they understand your situation.
5. Most importantly, you must understand the value of your own dreams and ambitions. While motherhood may be the most wonderful blessing known to womankind, but it is surely not the end of your individuality.

Historically, women have suffered oppression and domination by the patriarchal society in India and have faced many problems and challenges. Women were taught to accept their position through the socialization process and also that all rules and regulations made only for women they were bound to follow including their 'initiation rites.' They are taught to be obedient wives and sisters and also to respect their elders; manners are taught to them, like how to walk, talk, sit, work at home, and many others. They are neither considered as individuals with a personality of their own nor do they have any personal life. They are told that a man could marry more than one woman and they accept it silently, blaming it on their own fate. The inferior positions of women in traditional Indian society have been reinforced by a number of traditional practices such as polygamy, early marriage, illiteracy, and by years of subjugation. Many of these practices are still found today in some places in the country.

Participation of married women in prominent decision-making positions is limited by severe cultural and social constraints because men think that women are not capable enough to take a good decision. Women face challenges all over the world and sometimes these challenges are context-specific. The literature on the challenges and problems women face at the workplace is not only limited to women in the unorganized sectors but also informal organizations too, as women continue trying to contribute to their quality of life and that of their families and thereby to the economies of various countries through work. Women working in some industries, factories, banks, hospitals, etc. complain that they do not get time to look after and give care to their babies. The efficiency of a working woman is always suspected and questioned by most people, especially their male counterparts. In the upper-class cadres, it is generally seen that all qualifications remain similar, men are usually preferred. Authorities are doubtful whether women would be able to handle male subordinates, take independent decisions, cope with crises and manage their duties properly (Andal,2002).

It is a fact that married women have to face problems just by virtue of their being women. And if they are working the problems are multiplied manifold. Working women are those who are in paid employment. Social attitude to the role of women lags much behind the law. This attitude that considers women fit for certain jobs and not for other jobs influences those who are involved in the recruitment of female employees. For eons, the role of a working woman has remained constricted to the idea of a nurturer and a caretaker. She has not only been restricted to the domestic space of a household but has also been endowed with the responsibilities of taking care of her family and raising a child. Irrespective of her capabilities and her desire to shine in the public domain, she has to lead a quiet life playing the role

conferred upon her by society. However, with the changing times and regardless of all the prejudices they still face in their day-to-day lives, working women have started to take over the professional world and are seen thriving in many areas of work. That being said, although the number of working women has considerably increased in recent times, the problems faced by the same women have become a reigning public issue.

5

MISSING GIRL CHILD: FEMALE FOETICIDE- VIOLATION OF RIGHT TO LIFE

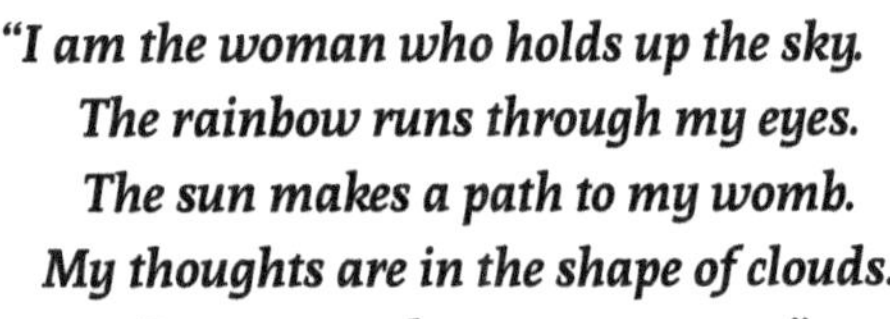

> *"I am the woman who holds up the sky.*
> *The rainbow runs through my eyes.*
> *The sun makes a path to my womb.*
> *My thoughts are in the shape of clouds.*
> *But my words are yet to come."*
>
> **(Poem of Ute Indians)**

These are the most striking and gripping verses of a poem in context to female foeticide. In a country like India where Durga, Saraswati and Kali assume a reverent position as symbols of profundity, erudition and might; where the womanhood is extolled and the mother is worshipped, the other side of the coin tells a completely different story. The female sex ratio has diminished progressively from 1901 to 2011 (Census of India, 2011). Towards the end of the 20th century, it was estimated that 37 million women were missing in India because of such pervasive anti-female practices(Sen, A., 2003). Statistics from the Census of India,

(2011)continue to demonstrate a decline in the female population, specifically in the 0 to 6 years of age. According to United Nations, report released in Jan, 2021, overall male female sex ratio of India is projected to decline at 103.36 males per 100 females in 2029(UNO, 2019). Even now millions of girls are missing in India.

Indian law recognizes the foetus as a special aggregation of cells with a potential for independent life and in this way protects the rights of **'unborn child'**. But even in modern times with so much progress and democratic setup, thousands of girl children are exposed to discrimination and violence in all settings in each and every part of the country. The height of this discrimination may occur even before they can see the light of day and continue beyond childhood into adulthood. The dwindling sex ratio, therefore, is a multifold blatant violation of human rights of a girl child. It is perhaps one of the worst forms of violence against women where a woman is denied her most basic and fundamental right-the right to life enshrined in Article 21 of Indian Constitution.The first, is denying the unborn girl child's right to be born and second is the violation of right to survive.It also negates the fundamental right to equality guaranteed under Articles 14 and 15 of our Constitution consequently, denies further their fundamental rights to the right to inherit, not to be harmed by drugs, dignity, self-value, education, access to medical care, services and information, to be involve in their communities or to express freely including denial of their most basic rights to name and nationality.

Further, it also violates woman's right over her body. Often the decision not to have the child is taken by the man (husband) or the family and the opinion of the mother who painfully bears the child, is rarely considered.

**Every dewdrop and raindrop had a whole heaven within it.-
Henry Wadsworth Longfellow**

Human rights are sure and sound assurance of democracy and may be regarded as those fundamental and natural or basic rights which guarantee the inherent dignity and worth of each human being. It assures that each human being born on earth will get regard, respect, protection, and will receive parental care and thus, ensures a decent life as human. However, through ages women have been suppressed and discriminated against in various forms and at different fronts on the pre- text of numerous socio-cultural norms, honour, traditions, customs, values and religious believes. The extreme form of this inequality and suppression is seen in not even giving her a chance to be born and cherish a dignified life.This also means that a large chunk of India's colossal population faces violation of human rights as gender selection remains a problem. It is calculated that India has the largest number of missing women (Grech, V. and Mamo, J., 2014) due to those patriarchal customs that perpetuate male preference (Sen, A., 2003), and promote selective elimination of females through practices such as sex-selective abortion(Patel 2013).At present the act of sex determination, sex pre-selection and sex-selective abortion happens with the intervention of a medical professional and the law is the only tool to regulate this intervention and prevent blatant misuse of medical technology.

The problem of sex determination, sex pre-selection or sex-selective abortion is rooted in many multifaceted bases and goes without focusing on the needs to address this predicament on priority. **'missing women'** victim of the most heinous and abhorrent practice of female foeticide is not just unfairness with a woman but also discriminatory when she enters what is often referred to as a **'man's world'**. Why is female foeticide practiced by some? The answer lies in a multifarious array of interconnected and intricate reasons, which probably have roots in socio-cultural fabric and further, have strong economic and other angles as well.

On probing into its reasons several facts that came forth, were not only shocking but horrendous and an eye opener to every one-

A. <u>Gender Selective Abortion: Unacceptable Logics and Paradoxes Explained</u>

Though it's a well-documented fact thatafter conception biologically women on the whole, are more resistant to disease and have better survival rates than males if given the same care as males. Considerable researches have shown that if men and women receive similar nutritional and medical attention and general health care, women tend to live noticeably longer than men. Despite this, at birth, boys outnumber girls everywhere in the world, by much the same proportion-there are around 105 or 106 male children for every 100 female children. In South Asia, West Asia, and China, the ratio of women to men is even low and varies widely elsewhere in Asia, in Africa, and in Latin America.Missing female births totaled around 30 million between 1980 and 2010, contributing to substantial deficits in the number of womenand had increased worldwide, from near zero per year in the late 1970s, to about 1·6 million per year by 2005 to2010.The situation in India is no better. As discussed in above sections, the scenario is grim if we see the statistics after 2010 to 2019-20 on Sex Ratio at Birth (SRB) which appears which is highly skewed. India accounts for almost half of global missing female births. In contrast to the substantial improvements in female child mortality in India, missing female births, driven by selective abortion of female foetuses, continues to increase across the states.The reasons given as under are not at all convincing for this crime-

1. Abortion through the Ages and Across Religions Considered as an Act of Crime

Every Human being including an 'unborn child' in the womb of its mother receives the right to life directly from the Almighty God but not from parents, society or any other authority.

Inherently induced abortion as such is considered as most appalled sin, a human may commit, in almost every religion on this earth.

Foeticide was prohibited and classified as murder in ancient Hindu texts and Hinduism. It was considered as equivalent to neglect of Vedas, incest, and drinking of spirituous liquors. In ancient India, man even considered a woman who had undergone abortion as murderer of her husband or of a Brahmin (*Brahm hatya*) or as an 'outcaste'. It is believed that the generations of the person who deliberately commits this ruthless crime, has to pay for it. The Buddhist, who condemned the destruction of life, laid down that Bhiku "who intentionally destroyed a human being by way of abortion, is no *Samana* and no more follower of *Sakeyaputra*".

In modern times, Mahatma Gandhi condemned abortion and called "abortion was more in violation of the principle of the 'ahimsa' than the artificial birth control which was morally blameworthy".

The 'Holy Quran' prohibits the killing of foetus. It says, "Astray have gone those who stupidly kill their children without knowledge and deny to themselves of what Allah has blessed them with".

The Didache, an authoritative source of Christian Law, considered abortion, as a grievous sin and was included in the 'Ten

Commandments', which contain the forbidden acts.

Thus, abortion is considered as one of the most abhorrent sins which is equivalent to deliberate killing of human beings, however, when it comes to gender selective abortion most people who favour this brutal practice forgo their religious dictums for their selfish motive.

2. Overall Sex Ratio vs. Juvenile (Child) Sex Ratio Unfavourable to Girls: Situation in India- Facts and Figures

The missing girls are clearly linked to their killing through sex selection. The statistical norm is to have at least 1,050 females for every 1,000 males. At birth, there ought to be around 105 or 106 male children for every 100 female children, and this proportion is about the same everywhere in the world other than some of the South Asian countries. Sex ratio at birth (SRB) is an indirect measure of female foeticide. The key factors responsible for SRB are female infanticide, sex determination and selective female foeticide(Mathew. S., Dec, 2000).

A consistent improvement is seen in overall sex ratio in India wherea marginal improvement of six points in the overall female to male sex ratio with 927 in 1991 as compared to 933 females per 1000 malesin 2001. The year 2011 again saw a rise of ten points i.e. 943 females per 1,000 males from the previous Census, 2001.

On the contrary, the status of juvenile or child sex ratio (0 to 6 years of age) is another story altogether. The child sex ratio has shown a steady and a progressive fall since 1961 and shows no signs of improvement. It has shown an adverse trend with sharp decline of 17 points from 962 in 1981 to 945 in 1991 in the country and a worrying 18-point drop between 1991 with 945 to 927 girls (an all-time low) 2001, a decade that saw a boom in the scan centre industry shows the gravity of the problem of extensive female foeticide in India. Though, little less but still worrisome 14-point drop with 914 girl children per 1,000 male children was seen in 2011 census. Same is the situation of Sex Ratio at Birth (SRB) in India.These data raises brows with worry especially because this particular ratio is the important indicator of nature of population and demographic pattern of the future of India and forthcoming problems related to this(Census of India, 2011).

As per NFHS-5-2019-20, (December, 2020) data the overall male female sex ratioat birth in the countrywasfound 929females per thousand males. Though, this is much higher than what it was in 2015-16 (919 female per thousand males) but is still low than the natural standard of 952 female births per 1,000 males.

In depth study of 2001Census shows that all districts in Haryana and Punjab are not only in D category (child sex ratio less than 900) but 25 out of 36 districts have child sex ratio less than 800 (D3 category). In fact, the 2001 Census showed the States of Punjab, Haryana, Gujarat, Himachal Pradesh and even Maharashtra having skewed child sex ratios falling below 800 girls for every 1000 boys. Among the worst affected were Mehsana (Gujarat) where the ratio is 798, Kurukshetra (Haryana) -770, Fatehgarh Saheb (Punjab)-754.

Indeed, the statistics are astounding. Numerous studies analyzing the skewed sex or gender ratio demonstrate the extent of this shocking practice. Figures of Juvenile sex ratio (JSR) are very important indicator and reflection of this discrimination. This can only mean one thing. More and more baby girls have either been aborted or killed as infants since 1961 and that this trend continues strong even today.

3. Rich vs. Poor

Unlike many other social evils attributed to poverty, the killing of female foetuses through sex-selective abortion cannot be attributed to poverty and ignorance. Surprisingly,sex selective abortion behaviour goes hand in hand with increased wealth. The situation is worse among rich and affluent population and better performing states. If statistics are anything to go by, the rich seem to be murdering their daughters. Desegregations of the Census of India, (2001) data revealed the disturbing trends of very poor sex ratio among the rich and literate. Earlier, it was thought that female foeticide and unwillingness of girls was more among the poor and the illiterate. Prosperity, intellectual or otherwise does not necessarily mean a change in social attitudes towards gender bias. Clearly it is those who can **"afford to choose,"**and use technology to do so.

The grim warning came 20 years ago in the 2001 Census itself that revealed a greater decline in sex ratio in the 0-6 age group too particularly in Indian States like Haryana, Punjab, Delhi, Gujarat and Maharashtra, which are prosperous, economically affluent or better off and the distinction of having more people who can pay for expensive tests to help choose male children over females. Some reports suggest a marginal improvement in the condition in Delhi but the reality is different in the posh colonies of South Delhi in particular.

The reason is simple. Women in the top wealth category have more chances to get the ultrasound checkups as compared to women from lower middle or lower wealth category.

The child sex ratio (0-6 years) in slum areas is 919 in 640 cities and towns in 26 states and Union territories, compared to 904 in non-slum areas, according to the data released by the Census of India, 2001.

Figures of juvenile sex ratio (JSR)or CSR (child sex ratio) showed much higher downfall in the economically developed States in India i.e., Punjab (798), Haryana (819), Chandigarh (845), Delhi (868), Gujarat (883) and Himachal (896).There is, further steep fall in sex ratio in districts of these States. Out of the 579 districts for which both 1991 and 2001 data is available, in 2001, in 477 districts more than 80% recorded a decline in the child Sex Ratio with most prominent in Gurdaspur (789), Sangrur (786), Kapurthala (785), Bathinda (785), Mansa (782), Patiala (777) and Fatehgarh Sahib (766) in Punjab(Census of India, 2001).

Demographers and activists have pointed out that sex selective abortions are rampant among well-off, higher caste and urban groups in Hyderabad.P. Balamba, former Superintendent of Nayapul Maternity Hospital of Hyderabad, speaks of leading doctors and film artistes getting sex selective abortions done(Aniket Alam,Dec. 20, 2003).

Indians in other countries are going for sex selective abortions are evident by the fact that sex ratio at birth among the Indian community in New Jersey is as bad as in Punjab and Haryana. The

British Law does not allow parents to choose sex of their babies except to avoid certain gender linked diseases. Abortion on the ground of sex is not allowed under the Abortion Act of 1967 in the UK. But sex can be disclosed by patients if they ask during ultrasound(K.V.Ramana Murthy, July 2006).

A report in the British Newspaper, 'observer', had come up with evidence that British Asian women go to India to abort their baby girls(K.V.Ramana Murthy, July 2006).

These statistics once again dispels the myth that poverty is responsible for sex selective abortions and highlights the adverse linkage between prosperity and sex selection.

4. Rural vs. Urban

It is interesting to note that urbanised cities are bigger culprits in this menace. For example, in Gujarat, Ahmedabad leads with child sex ratio of 809 per 1000 males, followed by Rajkot (821), Surat (830) and Vadodara (832). Ironically, districts like Mehsana (797), Gandhinagar (816), Rajkot and Ahmedabad enjoyed above average female literacy rate of 64, 65, 67 and 71 per cent respectively. In comparison, the so called backward, tribal districts of Dangs, Dahod and Narmada, with low female literacy rates of 49, 32 and 47 per cent respectively, have higher child sex ratios of 973, 964 and 952 (Census of India, 2001).

Though the urban child sex ratio has historically been low, the big fall in the rural areas is worrying as 72 per cent of the State of Andhra Pradesh lives in villages. Trends in the State of Andhra Pradesh suggest that this malady has spread to rural Andhra Pradesh where child sex ratio has fallen 14 points from 979 girls for 1,000 boys in 1991 to 965 girls in 2001. Social activist, Rukmini Rao, tells of tribal women who have taken loans from self-help groups to get a scan and sex selective abortions (Aniket Alam, Dec. 20, 2003).

The 2011 Census is giving a positive nod. Here the number of females per thousand males was recorded 7-point high (940) than the previous census of 2001 (933).

A comparison of rural verses urban shows skewed sex ratio in favour of males in rural areas of 14 States and in urban areas of 22

States whereas 06 States saw decline in sex ratio(NFHS-5-2019-20, December, 2020).

Thus, the disturbing fact is that these practices have been far more prevalent in the urban landscape than the rural countryside. Hence, one can infer that being from urban elite or educated background may not the perfect solution to the appalling reality of skewed sex ratio, nor may do wonders to the not-so-bright future.

5. Ordinal Position and the Number Game in Sex Determination

Usually, the earlier trend was that people use to go for scans and sex selective abortions after the first child was born girl but now, we are facing the tragic events of even the first daughter being eliminated in Punjab and Haryana. A desire for a son continues to remain strong among couples. Indirect evidence of this comes from analysis of the NFHS-2 data collected during 1998-1999 (NFHS-2, 2000).

This is a kind of gendercidethat people across cultures, caste, classes and communities are committing against a particular sex without thinking it long- term repercussions.

6. Discrimination against Women as Denial of Right to Survival at Various Stages of Life - A Life Cycle Approach

In many parts of India, the girl child is not valued and at every stage of her life, she may be discriminated and neglected for basic nutrition, education, clothing, health and living standard. Discrimination during different stages of life is another facet is making a girl child die even if she gets an opportunity to be born. This indirectly adds to high mortality rates of girl child. There are many inhuman forms of doing so such as killing just after birth by starving her and declaring that she was born still or dyed of diarrhoea or any other problem. Perhaps this is the reason why despite being biologically stronger than boys, a greater number of girl children die annually.

Further, disparities in the way girls and boys are raised and treated may lead to many sexual and reproductive health problems was found in a study in rural Uttar Pradesh conducted in 2004. Girls and women are more vulnerable to rape and sexual exploitation, to suffering from inflammatory diseases, urinary infections, gynecological complications, and are at high risk of contracting HIV/AIDS. Globally, young women are 1.6 times more likely to be living with HIV than young men. Particular concern is the dramatic increases in HIV infection among young women, who now make up 60 per cent of the 15- to 24-year-old living with HIV(Hitaishi Singh, 2004).

The harmful traditional practices include early marriage, early pregnancy, multiple and consecutive induced abortions at short intervals due to son preference, female genital mutilation, female infanticide, rape, incest, wife battering, dowry- related violence, trafficking, prostitution and the various taboos and practices which victimizes women just for being women and restrict her from exercising her human rights.

Overall, it is a vicious cycle that goes on and a girl foetus if given a chance to survive when get trapped into this cycle of discrimination and oppression, is never able to get out of it till her last rights.

B. The Root Causes for Discrimination in Form of Female Foeticide-TheVulnerability of a Girl Child

Women have been constantly being the victim of gender-based bias through ages in Indian society. The reason for this discrimination has kept on changing with certain causative factors dominant at one point of time and the other being subdued at the same time.These root causes for discrimination in form of female foeticide are complex and reflect diverse issues-

1. **Medical Reasons Related to Medical Compulsions vs. Lack of Medical Ethics- Two Sides ofthe Coin**

Many times, a woman is suggested by authorized medical practitioner to go for induced abortion due to several medical conditions and reasons such as life threat, or any non- curable abnormality in the foetus or as given in the PNDT Act of 1994 (and the modified CCPNDT Act),(Tabie Sheida,June, 2017). But there is the other side of coin too on the part of medical practitioners. These comprise mainly lack of medical ethics among some medical practitioners that leads them to run for the easy money making leaving behind all moral, legal and social obligations. Involvement of a large number of doctorsguided by prospects of making quick money and a lucrative business who have joined the race claiming to specialized in getting couples conceive male babies, and introduced mobile ultrasound facilities for sex selection or sex determination even in rural areas,further adds to this adversity. Many medical professionals actually believe that through sex-selective abortions they were instrumental in raising the status of the woman in her family and society by not allowing her to bear daughters.Others do so, on the pre- text of spreading family planning, thinking it to be a great social and national service. The medical professionals have, generally,so casual and indifferentattitude that they do not even bother to get their machines registered or make any attempt to maintain records. Knowing fully well that it is immoral, illegal and unethical as well as it may account to mortality or long-term morbidity of woman, foetus of a girl child is aborted by qualified and unqualified <u>doctors</u> or compounders and even by local '*dais*' in many cases.

In the recent years in spite of the declaration of sex determination as a punishable and inhuman offence, clinics, legal and illegal have sprung up all over the country in urban areas, and further penetrating to rural areas. These are carrying out female foeticide covertly and shamelessly.

The sanctimonious medical fraternity, in its unabated quest to accumulate wealth, has played a diabolic role. The opportunistic doctors have capitalized on the parents' anxieties and left no stone unturned in minting money. This only reflects the unethical and obnoxious face of our medical fraternity that is considered as next to 'God' by patients.

1. **Socio-cultural and Religious Reasons**

Researchers from King Abdullah University of Science and Technology (KAUST), Saudi Arabia, and Universite de Paris, France, in a recent study (Liverpool Layal, 2020),noted that there has been a reported imbalance in India in the sex ratio at birth (SRB) since the 1970s due to the emergence of prenatal sex selection and the cultural preference for male babies.

Further, as discussed above in the section of religion, deep rooted alliance of traditional thoughts as reflected in the 'son complex' unfolds the intricacies of the socio-cultural fabric of Indian society.This includes traditions and cultural values influenced by number of factors-

a. **The Devalued Status of Girl Child and Women vs. 'Son Preference or Son Complex'**

However, the sex ratio at birth (SRB) in India has become more masculine than the natural levels stemmed out of strong son preference. Son preference is stronger in countries where patriarchy and patriliny are more firmly rooted. The omnipresence of the mortifying truth of female foeticide or sex selective abortion can only be attributed to the patriarchal nature of Indian society that has nurtured the deep-rooted tradition of craving for sons. A hundred millionwomen who should have been part of this society have been denied a life because their parents wanted a son.

Findings from study by Hitaishi Singh, (2004)revealed that gender selection or in other words son preference was found to have a very strong role in family planning decision-making and is governed by the sentiments of both, husband and wife along with their family and community members. The research states that out of total 295 respondents 23 women had to go induced abortions with no reported reasons other than one respondent who did go for it for family planning reasons.

Countless reports the world over have demonstrated that in societies where son preference is practiced, the health of the female child is adversely affected. The practice denies the girl child good health, education, recreation, economic opportunity, violating her rights included in the Convention on the rights of the Child. There are instances like, leaving day's old girl-child near the gates of Governmental Health Centres, Juvenile Centres, Temples and Churches leaving <u>baby's</u> fate to God. Selling girl child for few hundred rupees to childless couples is another injustice to the girl child.

Satish Bansal, Co-Chairperson, International Union for Health Promotion and Education, Punjab Chapter (2003) highlighted the main reasons commonly put forward to explain the consistently low-level Sex Ratio are son preference, neglect of the girl child resulting in a higher mortality at younger age, female foeticide, female infanticide, higher maternal mortality, sex discrimination and male bias. They are generally the last to be educated or get medical treatment when ill.

In many areas of the country the desire to have a son is so strong that efforts to have son at any cost are made constantly, be it taking the life of a girl child or even the "import" of brides from outside their own states or communities. May be for some people this may not be a reality but this the existing truth of many parts of 21st century India.

b. Why Sons are Preferred over Daughters?

It is not a new thing for India. Indian families, traditionally have prefered boys because of the several reasons. Though these reasons cannot, in any way be justified for the killing of a girl foetus simply on the grounds of her sex but this is the harsh reality. The reasons for this practice may be many, ranging from emotional value, muscle power factor, economic reasons to socio- cultural roots. These identified reasons are described as under-

i. Son preference for family lineage

The social, cultural and religious structures and organisations of India are pre-dominantly patriarchal contributing extensively to the secondary status given to women. Baring few, ingeneral,Indian society is a patrilineal society where the family lineage is carried by male child. The family name is preserved through the son. The fear of losing the family name prompts families to wish to have a male child. The patrilineal social structure based on the foundation that the family runs through a male makes a male a precious commodity that needs to be protected and given special status. Another important pillar of the patriarchal structure is marriage wherein women are given subordinate status having no say in the running of their life or any control over their own body or bodily integrity. Even the girl takes her husband's surname name after marriage.

ii. Son as status symbol in the society and vs. son as a source of family strength and power in the society

Unfortunately, an irrefutable cause is the putative belief among good number of households consider male childasamatter of pride status symbol for the family. This feeling prevails equally amongst most backwards and elites of all classes, castes and religions in the country. More the number of sons one has, more powerful he is considered in the society and community.

For instance, though today women are also joining defense services but a common saying goes like 'a soldier's sons protect the community and country'.

iii. Son as old age security while girl as 'burden'

Sons have been traditionally a source of family income and social security. They are expected to provide physical, emotional and economic support to parents in their old age. In Asian region the birth of a son is welcomed with celebration, as an asset, whereas that of a girl is mourned and is seen as a liability, social responsibility and impending economic drain. They are seen as a burden on the family, requiring a huge dowry that many families cannot afford. The problem of safety of girls and the evil of dowry system has led to a belief that daughters have to be protected and sufficient financial resources have to be accumulated to support the marriage of the girl. Boys on the other hand are considered as assets, who fetch a fabulous dowry for the parents.

This has created a stereo-type notion of girl as a "burden" on the household.

iv. Son preference for religious reasons and religious hypocrisy

Widespread Hindu religious belief that only a son could perform the last rites when his father dies otherwise the father will not attain salvation or '*moksha*' is the major reason, at least in Hindu families in India. Situation has changed, but only at the superficial level with very few such cases where a girl performs last rites of her parents. Underneath the carpet, parents with no male child cannot expect to have an appropriate burial and secure salvation. This is an act of defying the very existence of his or her own biological child and is not fair with the girl child by any means.

Moreover, traditionally almost all religious ceremonies are performed by men or lead by men even if wife sits with him. Sons are the interpreters of religious teachings and the performers of rituals. Priests, Sheikhs and other religious leaders are men of great status, and this combined with religious faiths plays important role in forming wish to have at- least one male child in the minds of parents.

A powerful photo essay by G. SenRuhani Kaur (2003) highlighted the plight of women in different parts of Punjab, who were under constant pressure to bear sons. Local gurus made a pretty packet by selling all kinds of concoctions that they claimed would guarantee a male child, and quite often the result was a deformed baby.

Sadly, most religious gurus spent hours and hours in preaching how Indian tradition had always respected a woman within their own limited thinking often reflected when they talked about a woman being great **"because she is the bearer of sons"**, or **"without her a man cannot be born"** rather speaking on the greatness of woman's because she gives birth to life, of both boys and girls. This is the way of branding women with a label that decides the fate of their status in their respective families and society.

Perhaps this is the reason why everyone knows about the mother of Shivaji, or Maharana Pratap in detail but hardly knows about the name of mother of Rani Lakshmi Bai, Rani Chennamma.

v. Reasons, if a Girl Child is given a Chance to live are-

Evidences from a study conducted by Hitaishi Singh (2004), on 295 rural women from Uttar Pradesh reported that emotional reason or having daughter out of affection or emotional satisfaction (18.6%) barely find space in the reasons given by the respondents for having at least one daughter. Major reasons such as **help at home (**67.1%), ***Kanyadan***(60.7%), and tying ***rakhee*** to their brothers (30.8%) were given as reasons by total interviewed 295 respondents for having at least one daughter. A fistful wanted daughters as even after marriage they were found to be more caring and providing better old age security (4.4%) and as moral support for the mother (2.4%). In the same study reasons given for having at least one son were varied and the answers ranged from to continue family lineage (84.4%), for old age security (57.6%), economic reason help in farm, business and increases family earnings (29.8 %), religious reasons (for last rites of parents and inherit family property (26.4 %%), to increase family power in community, (21.7), help at home (20.3%), and emotional satisfaction (19.7).

Largely worth of girl child is accounted in social and economic terms. Out of total 114 (38.6%) of the 295 rural women not in favour of having even a single daughter in the family held single or more problems responsible for this answer. As many as 70.1% women accused dowry problem,40.4% difficulty in finding suitable match (husband for them), 16.6% safety of daughters and 16.6% not considering daughters as source of income or future security because they will become part of other's family after getting married as the reasons responsible for their opinion, said Hitaishi Singh (2004) in her report.

3. Socio-political and Historical Reasons

Female foeticide was not a regular practice in older times as it is today in India. However, practice of female infanticide was there which originally began due to certain socio - political and historical reasons. It came into practice in India majorly after frequent invasion from north-west frontiers other country and Islamic invasion to be specific to save the honour.Girls were considered as the symbol of honour of the family and any attack on their honour was not acceptable. After the war the victorious armies use to take their revenge on the defeated communities; women were ill-treated, raped, captured and sold or distributed as slavesto the soldiers and commanders of the winning army as part of the spoils of war. Subsequently, these communities resorted to killing their daughters at birth or when the enemy was advancing to prevent girls from the hands of enemy during the warfare and to spare the female population from shame that latter became a custom or mandatory act.

Under such circumstances, people use to relate males with muscle power and needed a greater number of males to combat constant wars. This deep entrenched son-complex in the Indian society, especially in the north-western states like Punjab and Haryana still exists, partly because of such historical reasons and can be seen in various forms even today.

Killing of foetus and infants takes placeeven now in the name of honour in many parts of country, especially Haryana and Western Uttar Pradesh. It is linked with dishonour the girl may bring to the father or the family when grows up.Parents have to bow their turbans or head in front of prospective bride groom's family in case of arranged marriages or while approaching for marriage or if she marries to person from other castes or religion or same *gotra* (clan)which is strictly prohibited in Hindus and their different cults or faiths (*panths*).

There have been innumerable cases of such inhuman and brutal acts of infanticide in the past. Traditionally the patriarchal families use to get rid of the "unwanted child" by using methods like starving her, poisoning, or letting her choke on husk, throat splitting, smothering and drowning or simply by crushing her skull under a charpoy. A commonpractice that still existsis disposing of girl infant, often in garbage dumps, where most die. These practices illustrate the insignificance accorded to the lives of the girl children that continue in a different form by taking advantage of advance medical techniques that has now taken the form of female foeticide.

4. Economic Reasons:

As far back as our history can be retraced, one can see that even the most primitive human rights of the female population have been squelched. In economic terms, it is a supply-driven phenomenon triggering off a large latent demand. The recent economic developments have done no good either. In fact, they have only added fuel to this seemingly eternal fire. Problem of dowry, inheritance and share in property on one hand and ability to pay the doctor and abortionist for the test and abortion with the increased income and buying capacity has led to the increased number of female foeticide.

In addition to this, people fail to foresee girl child as a potent breadwinner for the family. Rather, she is looked upon as a liability out of one which has to be paid as dowry. Even in today's **'New India'**, a dowry death is reported every 90 minutes and 19 women die or killed every day due to dowry (National crime Records Bureau, 2020).

In today's materialistic world where money and power are considered synonym to each other the worth of women is also seen in economic terms. She is considered as non-productive ignoring her sacrifices for the family and other invaluable contributions to the society and country. Therefore, efforts must be directed attitude and give women her due place and respect.

5. Technological Advancement: Boon or a Bane

Modern scientific technology and sex determination techniques have been in used in India since 1975 primarily for the determination of genetic abnormalities and to facilitate a series of pre-natal diagnostic tools to identify and cure any potential birth defects thereby ensuring the health of a baby. However, the advent, innovations and advancement of medical technologies has led to the revival and conversion of female infanticide into foeticide by highly misusing them, primarily to identify the sex of the foetus and subsequently selectively abort if the foetus was found to be a female. Increased and easy availability and accessibility to and knowledge of these modern sex determination techniques such as amniocentesis, biopsy, ultra sound tests, devised to detect genetic abnormalities along with trans - vaginal probes and in-vitro fertilization, which ensures that the new-born will be a boy, have further aggravated the problem.

This way, people have found new ways of satisfying their obsessions for son, especially in South Asia. Researches show that tests like amniocentesis and ultra-sonography, which were originally designed for detection of congenital abnormalities of the foetus, are being misused for knowing the sex of the foetus with the intention of aborting it if it happens to be that of a female (Patel, 1984).

This has affected overall sex ratio in various States of the country where female foeticide and infanticide is prevailing without any hindrance. Therefore, the cases of female foeticide were all time high in previous years.

Though Maharashtra is one of the most progressive states in the country in health, literacy, urbanization and socio-economic indicators but there also the declining trend of Child sex ratio can be seen. Maharashtra was the first State to enact PNDT Act in 1987, however, in a survey Maharashtra showed that an alarming 95% of the amniocentesis scans were being carried out for sex determination (Deshpande J.D., D.B. Phalke, V.D. Phalke, March 2009).

"In a study involving 70 women from different strata of society, it was found that 69 were aware of sex determination tests, 22 per cent had undergone the test and another 28 per cent had known someone in the family who has resorted to the test. This speaks volumes of the misuse of knowledge and technology even among the so-called educated class," says Trupti Shah of Sahiyar, a Vadodara based women rights' organisation (Manjrekar Nandini, Trupti Shah, October,2015).

Technological intervention and its misuse, raises certain pertinent and valid questions on the issue. These are- how, in which way and to what extent the interfacing technology has affected and is affecting redressal of-

- Issues of health and society,
- Misuse of medical technology,
- Social and demographic implications of misuse of such technologies
- Stakeholders involved in decision making processes of such technology interventions which can have far-reaching social effects such as decision-making process in family and society and women's role (or lack of it) in them
- Violation of the principles of medical ethics
- Issue of 'informed consent', patients' rights and doctors' accountability
- Ways to regulate the medical profession (especially reproductive technology) both internally and externally and limits to research and the techno-docs' power 'to play God'.
- Roles and limits of social legislation in tackling social problems
- Possible knock-on effects of the advent of New Reproductive Technologies (NRTs)-as Sex Pre-Selection Techniques (SPSTs), non-coital reproduction through IVF- ET or GIFF, surrogate motherhood to genetic engineering, etc.

Female feticide thus, is receiving fillip through misuse of technology, done surreptitiously with the active connivance of the service providers.The unacceptable, unethical,downright cruel and most heinous practice of female foeticide through pre-natal sex determination, sex pre-selection and or sex-selective abortion- a manifestation of the 'medical revolution' has thus, prove to be the modern adversary for the girl child or 'missing women'.

6. Improvement in the Quantity, Quality and Outreach of Infrastructure and Health Facilities

Easy availability and increased access to medical facilities and a good network of roads to cut down the cost and time of travel and made sex determination techniques easily approachable. Now the remote towns, villages and even tribal areas are well connected by road or train and scan machines have spread far and wide into these areas.

Clinics offering ultrasound scanning facility have mushroomed throughout the country, and despite making pre-natal sex determination a penal offence and appropriate signs being hung at these clinics, doctors and parents alike rampantly violate this law.

A study of Khammam district by Aniket Alam, (2003), revealed that thoughthe district had only 45 of the State's 2,025 registered scan centres, many mobile vans from Vijayawada tour villages in Khammam district offering sex determination tests for as low as Rs.100.

In many areas of Punjab there are commission agents who keep on wandering in remote areas for prospective customers and offer a package of services like taking pregnant women for sex determination tests followed by abortions of the female foetus for a meager sum of Rs. 500/ per case. The quality of services, health of the pregnant women and hygiene in such cases is never ensured(S. C. Gupta, 2003-05).

This practice is not merely the spread of a useful medical tool for providing better health facilities but these machines can and are to discover the sex of the unborn childand the fact was very well in the knowledge of general people.

These two cases also reflect that this practice prevailed across nation from north to the down south irrespective of communities.

7. Government Policies and Programmes: Support or Oppose the Sex Discrimination

Certain programmes and policies of the government such as the small family norms or the two-child policy has got mixed up with female foeticide and have gone adversely for the birth of a girl child. The preference for at least one of two children to be a boy, often leads to the second girl born to a family being treated far worse than her older sister. Over the years it has become quite clear that if people are forced to limit the size of their families, they prefer to do so at the cost of the life of girl baby. Family planning propaganda for the last five decades advocating a small family norm (two children) in the minds of numerous couples highlighted the urgency of undergoing such tests to ensure that ideally, there is one son and one daughter, if not two sons before one takes to sterilization. This is the most commonly popularized and advertised method of family planning.

With family planning programme launched in 1952 followed by two and further one child norm introduction of PNDT Act in 1994 and the modified CCPNDT Act 1996 was very late in terms of period. This wide gap of years between the two has successfully changed the demographic structure in many parts of country making it fatal for female foetus the most.

8. Weak Implementation of Laws

Although the judiciary has been playing its part, but proliferation of female foeticide even to the most insular regions has been observed. The Pre-conception and Pre-natal Diagnostic Techniques (Regulation and Prevention of Misuse) Act, 1994, prohibits determination of sex of the foetus. It also provides for mandatory registration of genetic counselling centres, clinics, hospitals, nursing homes, etc. Moreover, utilization of ultra-sonography, amniocentesis to determine and communicate the sex of an unborn is punishable under the law since January 1996.

Thus, in India, for example, infanticide was formally legislated against during British rule, after centuries of practice in some communities. However, recent reports have shown that there is a revival. Though misuse of amniocentesis is also prohibited, the problem is still prevalent in India.Lacuna on the part of timely legal intervention and weak implementation of laws on the part of administrators and implementers has been one of the reasons for its ineffectiveness.The focus has been only on the registration of the number of ultrasound machines and not on the actual act of abortions of female foetuses. Furthermore, in several cases the accused have not been booked under relevant sections of the Act. The liberal interpretation of the Abortion Act in India has also facilitated the spread of female foeticide and so also the ineffectiveness of the PNDT Act of 1994 (and the modified CCPNDT Act) and Supreme Court judgments to punish the guilty doctors(Tabie Sheida, June, 2017).

It is said that "justice delayed is justice denied" means if justice is given too delayed it is regarded as equivalent to denial of justice. Therefore, speedy and tough punitive action at both the endpoints, i. e.,on the individuals going for sex selective abortions and the medical person conducting such abortion has to be ensured.

9. Problem of Communicating the Messages Unambiguously, Effectively and Insufficiently

A mere statistical projection will not help us in understanding the social ramifications of female foeticide. Westill do not know how to communicate effectively with the masses. For example, the UN style of expression i.e., 'sex selective abortion' does not convey a sense of anger and moral obligation against this phenomenon whereas the Hindi expression *'bhrun - hatya'* (killing of the foetus) conveys a lot since it carries moral values as in case of genocide. It evokes a sense of guilt among the culprits and the masses towards the social evil.

Moreover, all our communication efforts have failed to even create awareness and generate correct and complete knowledge on the issue including legal provisions and related laws. A study (S.C. Gupta, 2003-05),highlighting the modus operandi of different diagnostic centers and nursing homes allegedly conducting sex determination tests and terminating female foetus in Punjab revealed that only 7% of the people had awareness about the PNDT act and around 30% of the pregnant women undergo sex selective tests in the district of Ludhiana and there was a steep rise in the incidence of induced abortions.

Another worrying issue is related to the communication of such messages in a way that do not create confusion among the masses or violate rights of women directly or indirectly in some or other way. For example, in case when the religious leaders condemn abortion because it meant the destruction of life it can act as a double-edged-sword. On one hand, while talking against female foeticide, it is told to people that abortions are *jeev hatya* and therefore should not be conducted. But on the other hand, the move will be misfired as it violates woman's right to have access to legal and safe abortion when she wants it.

10. Education and gender skew: Gaps

There are two dimensions of this aspect-

One, that is the more popular belief, opinions that since women are deprived of proper and quality education or education as such that hampers her overall development and independence, thus, makes her position weak in the society. This also affects her reproductive rights and right to keep or abort the child.

Contrary to the popular belief,Gita Aravamudan's (2007) research shows an adverse link between education and the gender skew. The more educated a woman is, the more likely she is to actively choose a boy, assuming that she decides to have one child. The only educated women likely to keep daughters are the very independent minded. Educated men, especially in the business class, also want to have sons to carry on their business.

The states that have not been victims of this social menace are Pondicherry, West Bengal, Mizoram, Kerala and Sikkim because of better education of women and the absence of 'sex fixation'(Census of India, 2001).

Gender discrimination replicates itself from generation to generation. If girls remain illiterate, they are likely to be less capable to raise healthy and educated families, to think and judge independently as well as to develop civic sense.

11. Effect of Economic Sustenance and Employment Status

A girl child rarely gets rest and recreation. From early ages girls from poor urban homes and rural areas are burdened by domestic tasks and child care that never ends. Compared with men, women have fewer opportunities for paid employment and less access to skilled training and are usually restricted to low-paid and casual jobs. India is an agricultural country and more than 60 percent of its population resides in rural areas where the main source of income is agriculture, its allied activities or cottage industries. Modernization of agriculture released the burden of tasks traditionally carried out by men leaving women's burden unrelieved. In some regions, the bias has led to shift from subsistence food (often women's crops) to cash crops (often men's crops). Although women contribute far more to the agricultural production, and several cottage industries including handloom and handicraft industries, they are by far largest group of landless agricultural labourers with little real benefits and poorly paid section. Many times their tasks are not even recognised and same is the situation when it comes to making decisions including child bearing decision.They have no say in major house hold decisions including reproductive health decisions and their rights.The systematic marginalization of women has led to an increase in violence against women including the practice of female foeticide.

C. Implications- and repercussions

The practice of female foeticide in Asia has been creating a worldwide demographic imbalance with important economic and social consequences. Sex-selective abortion has multi-dimensional detrimental effects on individuals, families, communities, society, and the future generations of female child or women. The far-reaching severe implications of female foeticide can be seen in various forms and levels-

- If this heinous practice of female foeticide continued then without any doubt it will disturb the balance of the male-female population in the future. The gradual fall in SRB (sex ratio at birth) or CSR (Child Sex Ratio) presents an alarming situation for the future of the country. It is a warning sign that indicates the imbalanced demographic structure and characteristics of future population of the country and the catastrophic implications we may have to face in long term.

- At the macro levels the fast-declining sex ratio of females in India in the future may adversely disrupted the social harmony and balance of the society and give rise to a state of anarchy. Further, such disproportionate sex ratios have diverse ramifications and increase in various forms of crimes against women such as increase in sex-violence and sexual offences against women, sexual harassment at public places and work spaces, abduction, rape, sharing of women within and outside wedlock,smuggling or purchasing of girls and general unrest among the people. The due to precipitous increment in the number of brothels, the problemof prostitution will arise at substantial scale and spell social disaster.This will, consequently raise greater safety issuesand create insecurity amongst common women.

- OHCHR, UNFPA, UNICEF, UN Women and WHO, (2011),showed serious concerns and conveyed dire warnings about the social fallout from the skewed gender ratio-girls getting married at younger ages, dropping out of school and dying earlier after being forced bear children when they are too young. It could also result in more violence against girls and women.

- In the most severe cases, discrimination against girls' children leads to death in cases of female foeticide, girl infanticide or neglect leading to death. Its magnitude on the women's health, are alarming. Consequences,such as psychological disorders and health hazards caused by poorly conducted sex-determination procedures, Illegal abortions- either self-inflicted or performed by unskilled birth attendants under poor sanitary conditions, mental turbulence and family pressure faced by women or even increased maternal mortality and morbidity as a result of multiple abortions are some to name.

- It is expected that shortage of girls may reduce the evil of dowry but on the contrary if there is a shortage of girls, the dowry system will not vanish and the status of women will not improve rather far from this happening bride price will emerge and men will have to 'buy' wives and a time will come when only affluent men will succeed in getting married.

- Experts also predict that due to forced polyandry, increased prostitution there will be respective rise of HIV cases as the indirect cost of female foeticide.

- **<u>Bride or Human Trafficking and Bride Purchasing-</u>**

As per 2013 UNDOC's Report, the demand for girls of marriageable age is so high that bride trafficking has turned into a thriving business in India.

Some Instances of the Magnitude and Seriousness of Impact from Evidences: The Heart Wrenching Facts

The ugliest face amongst all repercussions is seen in cases when the falling sex ratio often necessitated the purchase of a bride. These brides from Bihar, Assam, Manipur, Tripura and West Bengal, and even Nepal, are being trafficked to Punjab, Haryana, Madhya Pradesh and several other states of the country to fill in the shortage of women for marriage purposes. Once such a woman had borne a son, she becomes virtually a prisoner, and is not even allowed to visit her home State. Most ironic is that on the contrary, many times she is sold off to others, again, for the purpose of producing a son. Often these purchased wives are shared by all brothers in the family and the worst form of using them as a commodity is seen when she is shared by sons and fathers both. Women are bought and sold just as they were in medieval times. No one thinks about their continued anguish and misery. What kind of life do they lead, what is their psychological state and their future? Perhaps nobody thinks of that (Janmejaya Samal,2016 Apr-Jun).

An MP from Gujarat had narrated the story of a woman who was repeatedly sold every three years after she had given birth to a male child. (Janmejaya Samal,2016 Apr-Jun).

Dr. Madan Lal, Professor of Microbiology, CMCH, stressed that owing to decline in SR, Punjab and Haryana continue to exploit the girl child and threw light on the situations of women- and girl-child-trafficking in Northern India resulting in skewed SR. These trafficked-women are also exposed to domestic violence, sexual abuse and forced prostitution(Satish Bansal, 2003).

A Shocking Revelation on the Mindsets-An Example

The Bombay High Court, in a landmark judgment on September 6, 2007, found it *"shocking" that a couple from Andheri (Mumbai) moving the court could make such a submission that for a "less advanced society" like India where a "patriarchal mindset exists" and where a "girl child is not socially accepted", it is better that such children are not born. (This argument is also propped up by the notion that if you spend Rs 5000 on sex determination and termination of the female foetus, you don't have to spend Rs 5 lakhs on dowry for the daughter's marriage later.)*

In their verdict the judges, comprising the High Court's Division Bench, unequivocally declared:

"Sex selection is not only against the spirit of the Indian Constitution; it also insults and humiliates womanhood. It violates a woman's right to life".

The judgment further observed, albeit with a tinge of sorrow:

"It is unfortunate that people should be under the influence of outdated notions regarding sons versus daughters. As long as such notions exist, the girl child will be unwanted"(Mainstream, March,10, 2008).

Laws have, of course, been made stringent to deal with the problem keeping pace with technological progress. Yet illegal sex determinations and consequent terminations of the female foetus continue unabated. Therefore, honest implementation of Acts and laws is the need of hour. But at the same time a great deal of dialogue on the issue may yield better results.

The falling sex ratio would destroy the social fabric and thus it should not be looked only as a woman's issue but a pressing national issue. It is high time for the government to come up with a more stringent and punitive actions to curb the iniquitous act. Girl children need both preventive and corrective protection.

Following suggestions may prove to be beneficial-

- There is a need to tackle this problem on two counts-

- One, to talk to people about the merits of a girl child and insist on education and granting equal rights to women and the
- Second, there is a need to develop a social atmosphere where sex selective abortion or pre- natal sex selection should be considered more as an issue of morality than legality.

- The re-balance in sex ratio is impossible in the present social scenario unless a drastic socio-cultural change takes place in towards existing social value system and societal attitudes towards the girl child. We need to truly rid ourselves of this son-obsession and understand that our lives would be just as fulfilling even if we do not have a son.

- This also calls for empowering the women because until and unless they come to know about their rights, how can we expect them to protect themselves and their children from the atrocities.Considering the importance of promoting self-esteem as a prerequisite for the higher status of women in the family and the community.Governments must take effective measures to ensure that women have access to and have control over economic resources, including land, credit employment and other institutional facilities. Empowerment of women and measures to deal with other discriminatory practices such as dowry, etc. should be taken.

- Since female foeticide adversely affects the psyche of the woman on whom the abortion is conducted, the sooner the evil is buried, the better it would be.

- Universal birth registration, Registration of pregnancies, Registration of ultrasound clinics, collecting data on the status of the girl child, on still-born sex ratios and sex ratio of aborted foetus could help.

- Sex selection in the present context is a complex issue with several stakeholders - doctors, the government machinery looking after the implementation of the Act, health and women's groups and civil society at large. **Increased positive and constructive participation by government and judiciary-programme, policy and lawmakers, administrators and doctors- the implementers, civil society and other stakeholders is also recommended**

i. It is important to examine scientific, social, judicial, ethical economic and health consequences of the available new reproductive technologies.

ii. There need to be a stricter control over clinics that offer to identify the sex of a foetus and stronger check on abortions to ensure that they are not performed for the wrong reasons.

iii. Girl children are particularly vulnerable to human rights violations, simply because they are girls. They therefore require additional protections along with legal and policy reforms, existence of laws,heavy penalty and strict punishments, strong political will,committed administrative action in form of effective and timely enforcement. Gender-sensitive data collection and development of projects that improve women's health and expand their choices in life are also necessary.

iv. Doctors have a greater responsibility with an important and positive role to play and need to be more careful, vigilant, and morally oriented to curb evil. At the same time, a strong ethical code for doctors needs to be made and implementation of the same should be ensured. Doctors must also be sensitized and strong punitive measures must be taken against those who violate the law.

v. Unless various community-targeted programmes supplement it, a law in isolation is unlikely to make any visible changes to the present scenario. These community targeted programmes can be awareness building, counseling young married couple, keeping a constant vigilance against the practice of female foeticide. Again, much of these depend on uplifting the status of women in our society.

vi. A deleterious outcome of subjugated position of a woman is her vulnerability to violence, rape, and other forms of sexual abuse, dowry, trafficking, and demeaned social and religious value even within the family with little or no mechanism for combating problems. Keeping vigil by the task forces set up by communities. Child protection services at the local level must exercise special vigilance on the situation of girl children in every community. An alerting and protecting mechanism must emerge and operate at the local level.

vii. Government should mobilize all educational institutions and the media to change negative attitudes change negative attitudes and values towards the female gender and project a positive image of women in general, and the girl child in particular.

viii. Governments should provide shelters, counseling and rehabilitation centres for victims of all forms of violence. They should also provide free legal assistance to victims.

ix. In economic terms, as we have argued earlier, the phenomenon of female foeticide is supply driven. Then, what about the demand side? Obviously, the demand is for boys only. In such a scenario, there is a need to create a large demand for girls.As son preference is often associated with future security, governments should take measures to introduce a social security system, especially for widows, women headed families and the aged.

x. NGO's could play a role of prime importance in accomplishing the above objective therefore, more number of NGO's should come forward for the cause. Increasing awareness amongst the people through NGOs and other organizations may be useful. NGO's could commit themselves to address patriarchy, son preference as well as negative stereotypes and practices, and to empower girls to realize their human rights.

xi. The dominant role religion plays in shaping the image of women in each society, efforts should be made to remove misconceptions in religious teachings which reinforce the unequal status of women. Cooperation with religious institutions and their leaders and with traditional authorities is required in order to eliminate traditional practices such as female foeticide, genital mutilation, etc. which are harmful to the health and life of women and girl children. The religious heads should take up this cause as even today when a religious person says something, people listen; they listen to doctors but more to religious and spiritual leaders.

- Ensuring development of and access to good health care services by women along with simpler methods for complaint registration for all women, particularly those who are most vulnerable could help.

- Regular appraisal and assessment of the indicators of the status of women such as sex ratio, female mortality, female literacy rate,drop-out rate, economic participation and other such parameters of feminine importance must be initiated by the state on a more frequent basis.
- Negative portrayals and perpetuation of gender stereotypes by mass media should be stopped or at least avoided. Negative gender-based norms and practices may be transformed through educational, social, legal and other processes that promote equality of girls and boys.The challenge today is to initiate a vibrant, effective campaign against female foeticide with strong commitment to reach out to the hearts and minds of our people. Publicity for the cause through the media could be helpful. Mass campaigns and rallies for awareness, workshops, lectures, video spots, advertising and publication of articles are options.
- It is also essential to educate boys at school to respect, consider and even protect girls and women.
- Gender-sensitization training should be organized for all law enforcement personnel and such training should be incorporated in all induction and refresher courses in police training institutions. Since in the future the technology would move even faster than our imagination of catching its follies, therefore, the focus should be on understanding why sons are preferred over daughters, as well as developing effective communication strategies that would transform the social institutions that uphold son preference.
- All women aware of the problem should be called on to react against traditional practices affecting the health of women and children and to mobilize other women.
- Female foeticide should be treated as a crime and not just a social evil, therefore stringent punishment and punitive action are required.

- A joint report by OHCHR, UNFPA, UNICEF, UN Women and WHO (2011),calls for the need of specific researches. The report further states, Determinants and health and social consequences – all the determinants and consequences of skewed sex ratios must be assessed using different types of research, including qualitative studies that explore the contextual realities that underlie sex-selection motivations and practices, and their effects on different age and population groups.

A Ray of Hope

The genocide of girl child, which continues unabated in the country, had led to skewed sex ratio in the country up till 2001 Census. But the current data on over all sex ratio of India shows quite optimistic picture. NFHS- 2019-20 indicates that India has made significant strides in the last five years. In 2015-16 the sex ratio was just 991 females per 1000 males. India now, overall, has more women than men with 1020 females per 100 males according to latest round of NFHS, 2019-20.The initiatives taken and several reforms that were brought at the policy level along with the launch of result-oriented innovative programs focussing strategically on the empowerment and sustenance of women by the post- 2014 government has started ripping its fruits. These women centric schemes such as *Ujjawala Yojna, Jan- Dhan Yojna, Pradhan Mantri Awas Yojna, Kanya Sumangla Yojna* (conditional cash transfer schemes to support the survival and development of the girl child), *Jannani Swasthya Yojna*, and many more schemes that are not only focussed on providing facilities to women but also converting them as an asset to the family by making them economically empowered. These are just few of the host of such schemes.Government has also introduced social security system, and made several procedures simple such as scheme of widow pension and scheme for women headed families and the aged. However, it is just a good beginning; the struggle is long. Analysis of NFHS 2019-20 data shows that 13 States and Union Territories still have more males than females.However, a recent study carried out by researchers from

King Abdullah University of Science and Technology (KAUST), Saudi Arabia, and Universite de Paris, France(Liverpool Layal, 2020),estimated 6.8 million fewer female births will be recorded across India by 2030 due to sex-selective abortions.Thus, still there is a long road to travel to reach the goal.

Concluding Remarks

Women as section of society are particularly exposed to social, psychological, physical, mental, emotional and material risk and harm, including neglect. One of the principal forms of discrimination that has far-reaching implications for women is the preference accorded to a boy child over the girl child and low or no value placed to girls, subjects them to further exclusion, exploitation and violence and to the worst killing in the womb. Female foeticide is the worst form of negligence and non-recognition of the worth of any women as a human being. This is perhaps the reason why nowhere in the world anything like '**male foeticide**' takes place.

This is the crux of the matter that needs to be addressed forthwith.One of the greatest threats to our contemporary civilization is, thus, the menace of skewed sex ratio.

The problem of female foeticide in its latest version was presented in all its aspects by the Member-Secretary of the Maharashtra State Commission for Women who eloquently explained: "**The attempts at legitimizing the vetoing of female life even before it appears is worse than the earlier abortion related violence in the womb, precisely because it is so sanitized and relies on seemingly sane arguments against the policing of 'human rights' in a democracy in the intensely personal matter of procreation. This needs to be resisted at all cost**"(Satish Bansal, 2003).

A time has come when we must take the vow to preach and practice -"***A girl child is equally welcomed in the society and particularly in the family***" so that social and family harmony could be maintained.

Girl child – *the women of tomorrow- is the nation's asset and pivot for humankind should be given equal and equitable opportunities to develop as every citizen get, even more, as her development leads to the development of the society and further of the nation. If we can ensure this, we will be respected and remembered by our next generation for saving them from this* **"man-made catastrophe".***We must all work together to ensure that each and every baby girl is given her due. As* **Martin Luther King Junior** *has stated once,* **"The question is no longer between violence and non-violence; It is between non-violence and non-existence."** *fits completely on women in this case. Therefore-*

"Invest in girls, realize their value, help them realize their potential, let them live and bloom,"

6

DOMESTIC VIOLENCE AGAINST WOMEN MANY FACETS

You see things and say 'Why?';
but I dream things that never were and I say 'Why not?' "
George Bernard Shaw

Domestic violence against women is the ugliest face of attitude towards women in India. Some family sociologists and historians have perceived family as an arena of love, affection, gentleness, and a center of solidarity and warmth. They are immune to the stark realities of infanticide of girls, the anguish of widows, Sati custom, wife battering, and child abuse, and the recent phenomena of dowry deaths and destruction of an embryo of a female child. Whereas some Sociologists see family as a center of exploitation, assault, and violence, ranging from the punishment of children to slapping, hitting, homicidal assault by one member of the family on the other.

Family violence is not a recent phenomenon. Surprisingly enough, how is it, family researchers in India have not been attracted to this most vulnerable social problem? The paucity of research on intra-family violence can be traced to a number of factors. One of these seems to be the social definition of family as a non-violent unit. Family relations were seen being regulated by mutual sympathy, affection, congeniality, love, respect, and concern. Generally, we tend to overlook the violence which occurs in the family or try to repress the memory of it. The semisacred nature of family in our society has made the issue of family violence a taboo to be researched.

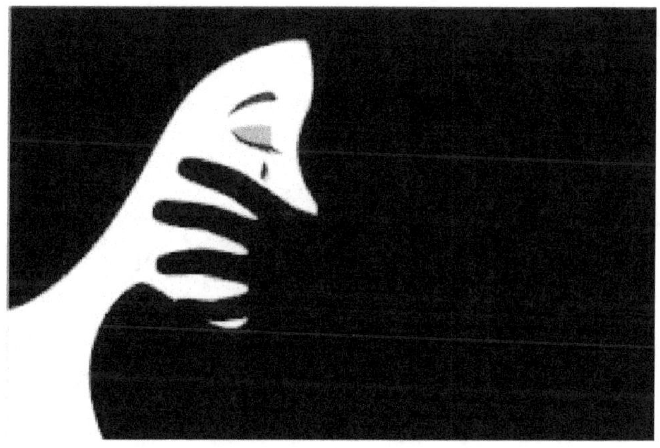

"Trauma may happen to you, but it can never define you." — Melinda Longtin

Domestic violence perpetrated by partners and close family members on women has long been mattering of silent suffering within the four walls of the home. The phenomenon of domestic violence against women has been identified primarily as a private concern. From this perspective, violence is seen to be a matter of individual responsibility, and the women are perceived to be the ones responsible for either adjusting more adequately to the situation as dictated by cultural norms or developing an acceptable method of suffering silently. This basic understanding of domestic violence as a personal issue has limited the extent to which legal resolution to the problem has been actively pursued.

Society has made the members of the family and elites believe that physical conflicts in the family are something other than violence. Violence in the family has not emerged as a social problem because social historians have not labeled it as a problem. The most important of all is the social dependency of women and children. Their low status and dependence are responsible for not giving air to their victimization, particularly in the absence of alternative social support systems. The women were trained to be 'make children', 'dutiful wives' and 'affectionate mothers'. Kautilya, Manu, and later Smiriti writers demanded from the wife not only to merge her individuality with that of her husband but also to accept her husband as god "Patiparmeswara" irrespective of the type of treatment she receives.1 Sati custom can be cited as an extreme case of exploitation and family violence. The son was expected to be obedient to the dictates of his father without even questioning his morality. The parents had absolute control over their children. The father had the right to mortgage, sell and even kill his children.

Domestic violence against women is increasingly recognized as a major health and social problem in India. Violence against women is widespread, deeply entrenched, silently borne, and relatively impervious to women's situation but male attitudes uniformly justify wife-beating and few would opt out of an abusive marriage. There is a dearth of information on the magnitude and patterns of domestic violence against women in India by way of community-based data. Facility-based data from police, court, hospital, and NGO records - do exist, but remain scattered, poorly maintained, and seldom used.

"Women, who know the price of conflict so well, are also often better equipped than men to prevent or resolve it. For generations, women have served as peace educators, both in their families and in their societies. They have been proved instrumental in building bridges rather than walls. They have been crucial in preserving social order when communities have collapsed. The place is inextricably linked to equality between women and men. To help ensure that women and girls in conflict situations are protected; that perpetrators of violence against women in conflict are brought to justice; and that women are able to take their rightful and equal place at the decision-making table in questions of peace and security".

Status of Women - Past & Present

Indian tradition in regard to the treatment of women is very complex, bristling with many contradictions, full of complicated adjustments and paradoxes of many kinds. The position of women during the Vedic age was in no sense inferior to men. She was respected and given more importance in almost all the fields of social life. It is believed that there were women warriors who were symbols of braveness, and equal to men. It is an open fact that there were women who distinguished themselves in the scholarly studies of Vedas and recited their hymns as also participated in public debates and discussions along with men. So, we can see that she used to have an equal opportunity to educate herself. In the rituals and all the ceremonies performed, women was having equal status. The Vedic term for wife "dampati" would suggest that the husband and wife were regarded as the joint heads of the households. It is also believed by the scholars that no low points of seclusion of women in Vedic society are seen. They could move freely in the company of friends and lovers. There are several passages in the Vedas which refer to love marriages. Women used to teach also in the Vedic period. Position in Vedic society was very well. She was adored, respected, and recognized. She had an identity of her own and received the same respect as was given to males. The value of law could not be denied in the Vedic society to the extent that sons were more useful to them than daughters. The position of women was different in Buddhism, which appeared in the sixth century B.C. Religion was more practical and elastic, as well as highly ethical. In Buddism, every human being - man or woman was a free agent able to work out his own salvation independent of any supernatural agency or the medium of priests for rituals. Nirvana, it is said, was possible for men and women. Brahmanism elevated the status of women. The inequality between men and women was wiped out in matters of religion: both sexes were charged with the duty of upholding Dharma. Hence, women with certain reservations in Buddism had a special place.

Violence against women affects women everywhere. It impacts women's health, hampers their ability to participate fully in society, affects their enjoyment of sexual and reproductive health and rights, and is a source of tremendous physical and psychological suffering for both women and their families. Recent research has shown that women who have been subjected to violence by their partners have greater chances of having a low birth weight baby, are at much greater risk of depression, and are more likely to have an induced abortion.

Socio-economic and political factors

Women are economically dependent on men, the social system to endorses this dependence. Men and women differ in their access to power, privilege, and prestige. The distribution of power as to who gets what, when, and how has traditionally been answered in favor of men. The work of the male outside the house has its worth and whereas the work of lady within four walls is uncounted for. If they want to work side by side they have to manage household also. The percentage of women who are having good jobs is very less. Even the voting behavior is dictated by the males in the family. A number of conventions have been signed regarding the upliftment of women and girls children. Yet a large number of women in the world are bereft of their rights. The reason is that they have not been translated to practice due to men, the dominant section of society.

Biological ideologies should not be allowed to prevail. The religious leaders and media which generally perpetuate such myths should be restrained from doing so. Problem lives in roots and foots these women must be made aware of their rights and be taught to respect themselves by caring about their own health and needs along with that of the family. Why is there so much gender injustice in India? In the 'Report on the Status of Women' published in 1975, it was pointed out that even though women constitute nearly half the population, they have all the characteristics of minority: inequality of class (economic situation), status (social position), and political power. The reason is not far to seek. Women do not constitute 'vote banks'. Their position would not have drawn even the meager attention it now gets but the international concern for the status of women.

Domestic violence Act

Domestic Violence means harming or injuring a woman in a domestic relationship. It includes physical, sexual, verbal, emotional, and economic abuse within its ambit. The abuse under the Domestic Violence Act includes not only actual abuse but also the threat of abuse. Any harassment resulting from unlawful dowry demands to the woman or her relatives is also covered by the definition under the Domestic Violence Act. The Domestic Violence Act primarily protects wives or female live-in partners from domestic violence at the hands of the husband or male live-in partner including his relatives. Section 2(a) of the DOMESTIC violence Act(1) defines "aggrieved person" as any woman who is, or has been, in a domestic relationship with the perpetrator and who alleges to have been subjected to any act of domestic violence. The Domestic Violence Act not only covers those women who are or have been in a relationship with the abuser but it also covers those women who have lived together in a shared household and are related by consanguinity, marriage, or through a relationship in nature of marriage or adoption including mothers, sisters or widows.

Types of Domestic Violence against women

The types of domestic violence against women range from physical, sexual, verbal, and emotional abuse to economic abuse.

1. Physical abuse: Physical abuse is the most prominently visible form of domestic violence against women. It has been defined in

the Domestic Violence Act to include any act that causes bodily pain or danger to life, limb or health, or development of the victim. Assault, criminal force, and criminal intimidation are forms of physical abuse.

2. Sexual abuse: Sexual abuse against women is in the nature of sexual/reproductive coercion. Generally, marital rape should come within the ambit of sexual abuse. However, marital rape is not outlawed unless the wife is below 15 years of age. According to the Domestic Violence Act, sexual abuse is any abuse of a sexual nature that 'abuses, humiliates, degrades or otherwise violates the dignity of a woman.'

3. Verbal and emotional abuse: Verbal abuse includes remarks/threats made by domestic relations during domestic violence against women. Verbal abuse further leads to emotional abuse and is an incredibly common form of domestic violence from the human rights perspective. The combination of verbal and emotional abuse leads to psychological abuse and erodes a woman's sense of self-worth.

4. Economic abuse: Introducing economic abuse in the categories of abuses under the Domestic Violence Act has been a remarkable step by the government. Economic abuse is generally characterized as a method of depriving or threatening to deprive the victim and her children of the use of financial resources/assets.

Causes of Domestic Violence in India

There is no uniform or single reason that leads to domestic violence. It is a combination of various sociological/behavioral, historical, religious, and cultural factors that lead to the perpetration of domestic violence against women.

1. Sociological/Behavioral Factors: The sociological, behavioral, and cultural factors include factors like anger issues/aggressive attitude, poverty/economic hardship, the difference in status, controlling/dominating nature, drug addiction, upbringing, and

psychological instability (bipolar, depression, stress, etc.) among others. Neglect of conjugal responsibilities due to extra-marital affairs or lack of trust also contributes to domestic violence.

2. Historical Factors: Historical factors can be traced back to the inherent evil of patriarchy and superiority complex that has prevailed for centuries among men.

3. Religious Factors: A subtle form of domination on women, if not direct and glaring, reflects in the religious sanctifications. This also contributes to the perpetration of domestic violence against women.

4. Cultural Factors: Cultural Factors leading to domestic violence include the desire for a male child. This obsession resulting from the lack of awareness and inherent male superiority leads to the perpetration of domestic violence against women. This is not an exhaustive list of factors and the motivations or triggers behind domestic violence may vary.

5. Dowry: A dowry is a form of socio-cultural factor. But, it becomes important to separately mention it because of the rampant domestic violence cases resulting from illegal demand of dowry. This was realized by the Parliament also because dowry-related domestic violence has been made a separate head in the scope of abuse resulting in domestic violence under the Domestic Violence Act.

One in three women worldwide experiences physical or sexual violence, mostly by an intimate partner. Violence against women and girls is a human rights violation, and the immediate and long-term physical, sexual, and mental consequences for women and girls can be devastating, including death. Violence negatively affects women's general well-being and prevents women from fully participating in society. It impacts their families, their community, and the country at large. It has tremendous costs, from greater strains on health care to legal expenses and losses in productivity. At least 155 countries have passed laws on domestic violence, and 140 have legislation on sexual harassment in the

workplace (World Bank 2020). But challenges remain in enforcing these laws, limiting women and girls' access to safety and justice. Not enough is done to prevent violence, and when it does occur, it often goes unpunished. Under the Domestic Violence Act, any woman who is aggrieved or anyone who has been a witness to the act can approach the nearest Police Station, Protection Officer and Service Provider. The court can appoint a protection officer to enforce its orders. The protection officer is a special post created to serve as a liaison between victims of domestic violence and the system. r One can also file a complaint directly with the magistrate for obtaining orders of relief under the Domestic Violence Act. Anyone who provides information about the offense committed to the concerned authorities is absolved of any civil/ criminal liability. The formation of a pattern of abuse is the characteristic feature of domestic violence. There remains a constant need and a constant effort to maintain power and control over the other, leading to a systematic pattern of power and control perpetrated by one intimate partner against another. In contrast, situational violence occurs when both the partners confront conflict with violence against each other and are specific to a particular situation. Situational violence occurs less frequently than domestic violence. Unlike situational violence, domestic violence happens frequently and has a tendency to result in long-term physical, emotional and psychological harm or even worse, death.

7
ACID ATTACK ON WOMEN: A COWARDLY CRIME

You don't just stumble into the future.
You create your own future.

Roger Smith

Women are an important part of our society. Every woman has her own job or duty in this modern society in which men are unfortunately still the 'strongest gender', we can't forget that a woman´s life is a lot more complicated than a man's life. A woman has to take care of her own personal life and if she is a mother, she has to take care also of her children´s lives too. Worse still, if she is married, additional stress can be on her shoulders. Yet they will still perform very well in the work environment in some cases better than their male counterparts. "Violence against women is a manifestation of historically unequal power relations between men and women, which have led to domination over and discrimination against women by men and to the prevention of the full advancement of women. Gender-based violence is endemic worldwide, cutting across age, marital status, religion, class, race, and thus poses human rights violations and huge health problems. In this paper, the focus will be given only to acid attacks, especially in India.

Often a crime of honour, acid violence is an inhuman crime which can be viewed to mean the deliberate use of throwing premeditated acid to attack another human being. The National Commission of India defined acid attack as "any act of throwing acid or using acid in any form on the victim with the intention of or with knowledge that such person is likely to cause to the other person permanent or partial damage or deformity or disfiguration to any part of the body of such person".

In a study conducted by UNICEF reveals, "Acid attack is a serious problem all over the world, even children are become victim of acid attack in many cases. In an Acid attack, acid is thrown at the face or body of the victim with deliberate intent to burn and disfigure. Most of the victims are girls, many below the age of 18, who have rejected sexual advances or marriage proposals. Acid attack or vitriolage is defined as the act of throwing acid onto the body of a person "with the intention of injuring or disfiguring [them] out of jealousy or revenge". The most common types of acid utilized in these assaults include sulphuric, nitric, and hydrochloric acid. Attack through acid rarely kills but it causes severe physical, psychological and social scarring. The victims of acid violence are overwhelmingly women and children, and attackers often target the head and face in order to maim, disfigure and blind a person for life and push her in everlasting life of pain and apathy.

An acid attack involves the premeditated throwing of acid on a victim, usually on her face. It is a gender-based heinous crime against women. In addition to causing psychological trauma, acid attacks result in severe pain, permanent disfigurement, subsequent infections, often blindness in one or both eyes. According to the National Commission of India, an acid attack is "any act of throwing acid or using acid in any form on the victim with the intention of or with the knowledge that such person is likely to cause to the other person permanent or partial damage or deformity or disfiguration to any part of the body of such person". Acid attack on women is increasing day by day, basically on the girls in the age of 11-30 years.

The most common types of acid utilized in these assaults include sulphuric, nitric, and hydrochloric acid. . Several community awareness programs are being conducted by local authorities and administrative departments, to make people aware of this heinous crime. Acid attacks cause severe bodily pain and life-long psychological trauma by shattering their primary physical/social identity in an instant (Anwary, 2019), which often makes them a subject of pity. Indian law does not contain an exhaustive legal definition for acid attacks, but the crime generally involves the throwing, spraying, or pouring of acid on a person's body or face with an intention to cause bodily or facial disfigurement or death. Acids are corrosive substances that have the potential to burn and severely scar everything they touch. The most common type of acids (tezaab in India) used in acid attacks are sulfuric acid, nitric acid, and hydrochloric acid, all of which are generally used for cleaning, manufacturing of cotton and rubber, and other industrial purposes.

"When it comes to abuse, you believe there's no way out. There is always help. There is always a way out." — Rev. Donna Mulvey

1. As per the provision of the "Prevention of Offences (by Acids) Act 2008,(National Commission for Woman – Draft Bill)" constitute the definition of Acid Attacks and Acid.

2. According to Section 3 of said Act:"Acid" shall mean and includes any substance which has the character of acidic or corrosive or burning nature that is capable of causing bodily injuries leading to scars or disfigurement or temporary or permanent disability.

3. "Acid attack" means any act of throwing acid or using acid in any form on the victim with the intent of or with the knowledge that such person is likely to cause to the other person Permanent or partial damage or deformity or disfiguration to any part of the body of such person.

Any country indicates a country's failure to protect its constituents from this specific harm. Several countries including India have adopted stringent measures to eradicate acid attacks, and many have been successful. In India, however, the measures have had little to no effect. In India, acid attacks are a gender-based crime, often associated with relationship, marriage, or dowry issues. This contrasts with the United Kingdom where males are the usual victims, and where attacks usually result from gang-based activities. In either case, the attacks are designed to seriously hurt and main victims, rather than kill them, thus causing significant and protracted physical and emotional suffering.

EFFECT OF ACID ATTACKS

Acid has a devastating effect on the human body, often permanently blinding the victim. The aftermath being the inability to do many everyday tasks such as working and even mothering are rendered extremely difficult if not impossible. According to the Acid Survivors Foundation in Pakistan, there is a high survival rate amongst victims of acid attacks. Consequently the victim is faced with physical challenges, which require long term surgical treatment, as well as psychological challenges, which require indepth intervention from psychologists and counsellors at each stage of physical recovery. The victims are often left with no legal recourse, limited access to medical or psychological assistance, and have no means to support themselves .

1. PHYSICAL - Acid eats through two layers of the skin, i.e. the fat and muscle underneath, and sometimes not only eats through to the bone but even dissolve the bone. The deepness of injury totally depends on the strength of the acid and the duration of its contact with the skin. When thrown on a person's face, acid rapidly eats into eyes, ears, nose and mouth. Eyelids and lips may burn off completely. The nose sometimes melts, closing the nostrils, and ears shrivel up. Acid can quickly destroy the eyes, blinding the victim. Skin and bone on the skull, forehead, cheeks and chin may dissolve. When the acid splashes or drips over the neck, chest, back, arms or legs, it burns everywhere it touches. The biggest immediate danger for victims is breathing failure. Inhalation of acid vapors can create breathing problems in two ways: i) By causing a poisonous reaction in the lungs. ii) By swelling the neck, which constricts the airway and strangles the victim When the burns from an acid attack heal, they form thick scars which pull the skin very tight and can cause disfigurements. For instance, eyelids may no longer close, the mouth may no longer open; and the chin becomes welded to the chest .

2. PSYCHOLOGICAL - Acid assault survivors face many mental health issues upon recovery. Acid violence victims have been reported with higher levels of anxiety, depression, due to their appearance. According to the Rosenberg Scale, the women reported lowered self esteem and increased self consciousness, both in general and in the social sphere.

3. SOCIAL AND ECONOMIC - Acid attacks usually leave victims handicapped in some way, rendering them dependent on either their spouse or family for everyday activities, such as eating and running errands. They face a lifetime of discrimination from society and they become lonely. These dependencies are increased by the fact that many acid survivors are not able to find suitable work, due to impaired vision and physical handicapped. As a result, divorce, abandonment by husbands is common in the society.

Moreover, acid survivors who are single when attacked almost certainly become ostracized from society, effectively ruining marriage prospects. They are embarrassed that people may stare or laugh at them and may hesitate to leave their homes fearing an adverse reaction from the outside world. Victims who were not married are not likely to get married and those victims who have got serious disabilities because of an attack, like blindness, will not find jobs and earn a living. Discrimination from other people, or disabilities such as blindness, makes it very difficult for victims to fend for themselves and they become dependent on others for food and money

LEGAL EFFECT OF ACID ATTACK

The Indian Penal Code, 1860 by virtue of Criminal Law (Amendment) Act, 2013 under the Explanation 1 of Section 326B has defined acid to include: "any substance which has the acidic or corrosive character or burning nature, capable of causing bodily injury leading to scars or disfigurement or temporary or permanent disability". National Commission of India, July 2009, Acid attack can be perceived as "any act of throwing acid or using acid in any form on the victim with the intention of or with the knowledge that such person is likely to cause to the other person permanent or partial damage or deformity or disfiguration to any part of the body of such person.

In India, often incidences of acid attacks grab the headlines of Indian media. Unfortunately in India, there was no separate legislation to deal with acid attacks before the passing of The Criminal Law (Amendment) Act. 2013. The offence was registered under Sections 320, 322, 325, 326 and 307 of the Indian Penal Code (I.P.C).

SECTION 320 - GRIEVOUS HURT - The following kinds of hurt only are designated as "grievous":- Firstly- Emasculation Secondly - Permanent privation of the sight of either eye. Thirdly - Permanent privation of the hearing of either ear, Fourthly - Privation of any member or joint. Fifthly - Destruction or permanent impairing of the powers of any member or joint. Sixthly - Permanent disfiguration of head or face. Seventhly - Fracture or dislocation of a bone or tooth Eighthly - Any hurt which endangers life or which causes the sufferer to be during the space of twenty days in severe bodily pain, or unable to follow his ordinary pursuits.

SECTION 322 - VOLUNTARILY CAUSING GRIEVOUS HURT - Whoever voluntarily causes hurt, if the hurt which the intends to cause or knows himself to be likely to cause is grievous hurt, and if the hurt which he causes is grievous hurt, is said to "voluntarily to cause grievous hurt. Explanation. - A person is not said voluntarily to cause grievous hurt except when he both causes grievous hurt and intends or knows himself to be likely to cause grievous hurt. But he is said voluntarily to cause grievous hurt, if intending or knowing he to be likely to cause grievous hurt of one kind; he actually causes grievous hurt of another kind.

SECTION 325 - PUNISHMENT FOR VOLUNTARILY CAUSING GRIEVOUS HURT Whoever, except in the case provided for by section 335(Voluntarily causing grievous hurt on provocation), voluntarily causes grievous hurt, shall be punished with imprisonment of either description for a term which may extend to seven years, and shall also be liable to fine.

SECTION 307 - ATTEMPT TO MURDER - Whoever does any act with such intention or knowledge, and under such circumstances that, if he by that act caused death, he would be guilty of murder, shall be punished with imprisonment of either description for a term which may extend to ten years, and shall also be liable to fine; and if hurt is caused to any person by such act, the offender shall be liable either to imprisonment for life, or to such punishment as is hereinbefore mentioned. Attempts by life convicts - When any person offending under this section is under sentence of imprisonment for life, he may, if hurt is caused, be punished with death. On 2nd April 2013 the Indian Penal Code was amended with the passing of 'The Criminal Law (Amendment) Act, 2013. The amendment resulted in insertion of Sections 326A and 326B specifically for dealing with acid violence.

SECTION 326 A states – Whoever causes permanent or partial damage or deformity to, or burns or maims or disfigures or disables, any part or parts of the body of a person or causes grievous hurt by throwing acid on or by administering acid to that person, or by using any other means with the intention of causing or with the knowledge that he is likely to cause such injury or hurt, shall be punished with imprisonment of either description for a term which shall not be less than ten years but which may extend to imprisonment for life, and with fine.

SECTION 326 B states – Whoever throws or attempts to throw acid on any person or attempts to administer acid to any person, or attempts to use any other means, with the intention of causing permanent or partial damage or deformity or burns or maiming or disfigurement or disability or grievous hurt to that person, shall be punished with imprisonment of either description for a term which shall not be less than five years but which may extend to seven years, and shall also be liable to fine.

COMPENSATION FOR ACID ATTACK

SECTION 357 C has been newly inserted whereby all hospitals, public or private are required to provide first aid or medical treatment free of cost. The section reads as: "All hospitals, public or private, whether run by the Central Government, the State Government, local bodies or any other person, shall immediately, provide the first-aid or medical treatment, free of cost, to the victims of any offence covered under section 326A, 376, 376A, 376B, 376C, 376D or section 376E of the Indian Penal Code and shall immediately inform the police of such incident." Apart from the above legislations, The Supreme Court of India has given state authorities three months to implement new rules to control over-the-counter sales of acids, which have been used to disfigure, maim and even kill people, particularly women, for decades.

No doubt, women are being heard and movies like Chhapaak are being made, the respect that women deserve is far from their reach. Chhapaak was inspired by the story of Laxmi Agarwal, who was burnt with acid in Delhi in 2005 when she was barely 15 years of age.

She protests banning the sale of acid in India and supporting acid attack survivors. Many other acid attack victims are working for this cause, to save other girls from such heinous, heart-rendering incidents. "Question is why and who do we have to save our girls from? We need to save them from the males who undergo rejection, of their friendship, marriage, dating, and sexual proposals. Why is the male ego so poisonously dangerous that it cannot stand a no and take vengeance and revenge from innocent girls, by throwing acid on their faces. The ideology or the thought remains that, 'what can't be mine, can't be anyone else's either. It only shows their disturbed and harmful psyche,".

Women constitute an important part in the society. They are responsible for giving birth to a life but unfortunately, they are made to lose their lives in name of different brutalities committed against them. Whenever a woman decides to raise her voice against her substandard position in the patriarchal society, she is shunned by different means; either by acid, physical abuse or by burning her to death. India tragically tops the global charts when it comes to acid attacks targeting women. Despite stricter laws and harsher punishments, the number of such attacks continues to increase on the subcontinent. The low conviction rate is also not helping the cause. Section 326 A in the Indian Penal Code lays down the punishment for acid attacks. The minimum punishment is 10 years' imprisonment. It can extend up to life imprisonment with a fine. A separate law to punish offenders in such cases was passed along with an amendment of the law on sexual offenses, in 2013, after the PIL filed by Laxmi Agarwal a victim of acid attacks. "These perpetrators should be punished vehemently, and stricter laws and penalties should be imposed on such wrongdoers, who destruct and devastate the lives attacking them with acids. Experts feel that fast track courts should be constituted to adjudicating, these matters , India's population is humungous and so are the number of cases, more fast track courts should adjudicate these matters, so that punishments could be imposed and justice should prevail. "Section 326 A & 326 B should

be imposed per the prevailing law, and Indian Penal Code. Also there should be awareness workshops conducted by NGO and on social media, awareness sessions should be conducted to cease and control the increasing aggression and frustrated instincts in the males, they should be educated to accept a rejection, or no. Human values need to be imbibed in them, they need to be properly trained that females are not their property. Human life is precious.

ppp

8

SEXUAL ABUSE AGAINST WOMEN - A COMMON PRACTICE

Keep me away from the wisdom which does not cry,
the philosophy which does not laugh and the greatness
which does not bow before children.

Kahlil Gibran

Sexual Abuse and Sexual Haressement are two sides of the same coin. Both showcase the power of men to dominate that of women. Both have one victim- a woman. Both are barbaric in nature; but many people extenuate sexual harassment to rape, just because the victims are not physically harmed. Whereas in rape- the victim is ravished like an animal for the fulfillment of desire and lust of another man. Both have the same object- to undermine the integrity of the victim, physically as well as mentally.

How is Sexual Harassment defined under the IPC?

Sexual harassment is defined under S. 354 A of the IPC as a man committing any of the following acts:

- **(i) physical contact and advances involving unwelcome and explicit sexual overtures; or**
- **(ii) a demand or request for sexual favors; or**

- **(iii) showing pornography against the will of a woman; or**
- **(iv) making sexually colored remarks,**

Sexual assault can be verbal, visual, or anything that forces a person to join in unwanted sexual contact or attention. Examples of this are voyeurism (when someone watches private sexual acts), exhibitionism (when someone exposes him/herself in public), incest (sexual contact between family members), and sexual harassment. It can happen in different situations, by a stranger in an isolated place, on a date, or in the home by someone you know.

**"Each time a woman stands up for herself without knowing it possibly, without claiming it, she stands up for all women." —
Maya Angelou**

1. **Nearly 1 in 5 women have experienced completed or attempted rape during their lifetime.**
2. **1 in 3 female rape victims experienced it for the first time between 11-17 years old.**
3. **1 in 8 female rape victims reported that it occurred before age 10.**

Sexual assault and abuse is any type of sexual activity that you do not agree to, including:

1. **Rape—sexual intercourse against a person's will**
2. **Forcible sodomy—anal or oral sex against a person's will**
3. **Forcible object penetration—penetrating someone's vagina or anus, or causing that person to penetrate her or himself, against that person's will**
4. **Marital rape**
5. **Unwanted sexual touching**
6. **Sexual contact with minors, whether consensual or not**
7. **Incest (Sexual intercourse or sexual intrusion between family members.)**
8. **Any unwanted or coerced sexual contact**

Sexual violence (SV) refers to sexual activity when consent is not obtained or not freely given. SV impacts every community and affects people of all genders, sexual orientations, and ages. Anyone can experience SV, but most victims are female. SV affects millions of people each year in the United States. The official numbers are likely an underestimate because many cases go unreported. Victims may be ashamed, embarrassed, or afraid to tell the police, friends, or family about the violence.

Sexual violence is a major problem faced by women and girls in India. It is already a challenge for survivors to obtain justice in the Indian legal system, and those from the country's marginalized communities face even more major barriers. There were 32,033 reported rape cases in 2019, with 33,356 in 2018. According to official crime data, there were 3,486 reported cases of rape against Dalit (Scheduled Caste) women and girls in 2019, and 1,110 reported rape cases against Adivasi women and girls (Scheduled Tribes). Survivors of sexual violence face huge barriers in accessing justice, including community pressure to drop the case, discriminatory attitudes of police and judicial officers, insufficient legal aid, and discouraging conviction rates. These challenges are often magnified if the survivors are members of India's marginalized communities, particularly if they are Dalits, Adivasis, or Muslims.

Sexual violence is a crime rooted in control and patriarchy, including male entitlement. In India, society often still shifts blame onto survivors, shaming a survivor and her family into silence. This is especially true among those who are already marginalized within Indian society, leaving them particularly vulnerable to sexual violence. This culture of shame follows survivors into law enforcement, the court system, and hospitals, further silencing survivors' voices.

DEFINE DIFFERENT FORMS OF SEXUAL ABUSE

1. Stranger Rape:Is rape or sexual assault perpetrated by someone unknown to the survivor.
2. Blitz Sexual Assault:The perpetrator rapidly and brutally assaults the victim with no prior contact. Blitz assaults usually occur at night in a public place.
3. Contact Sexual Assault:The perpetrator works to gain trust and confidence before assaulting.
4. Home Invasion Sexual Assault:Perpetrator breaks into survivors home to commit the assault.
5. Acquaintance Rape:Is an umbrella term used to describe sexual assaults in which the survivor and the perpetrator are known to each other, whether by passing acquaintance or someone the survivor knows intimately. This is the most common form of rape.
6. Child Sexual Abuse:Is a form of child abuse that includes sexual activity with a minor. A child cannot consent to any form of sexual activity, period. When a perpetrator engages with a child this way, they are committing a crime that can have lasting effects on the victim for years. Child sexual abuse does not need to include physical contact between a perpetrator and a child. Some forms of child sexual abuse include: Obscene phone calls, text messages, or digital interaction; Fondling; Exhibitionism, or exposing oneself to a minor; Masturbation in the presence of

a minor or forcing the minor to masturbate; Intercourse; Sex of any kind with a minor, including vaginal, oral, or anal; Producing, owning, or sharing pornographic images or movies of children; Sex trafficking; Any other sexual conduct that is harmful to a child's mental, emotional, or physical welfare.

7. Statutory Rape:Is defined as unlawful intercourse with a minor, California law mandates that an adult cannot have sex with a minor, and a minor cannot have sex with another minor, even if the intercourse was consensual.

8. Spousal/Partner Rape:Is between two individuals who are in a relationship. Sexual violence often works alongside among abusive behavior. Women who have been physically abused by their partner have often experienced sexual abuse, and haven't disclosed or did not realize sexual violence does not always include physical violence, making it difficult to acknowledge the abuse.

9. Incest:Is defined as sexual abuse by a relative, sexual contact/ abuse between family members.

10. Serial Rape:Is the most frequently sensationalized form of rape. Because of the frequently gruesome nature of the assaults and because of the opportunity to prey on people's fears, serial rape is frequently covered extensively by the media. The term serial rape is used to describe a series of rapes committed on different occasions by the same perpetrator. An important distinction is that this term is rarely used to describe marital or date rape, even though these types of rapes can happen repeatedly. Instead, the serial rapist has multiple victims.

11. Substance Facilitated Rape:Occurs when alcohol or drugs are used to compromise an individual's ability to consent to sexual activity. These substances make it easier for a perpetrator to commit sexual assault because they inhibit a person's ability to resist and can prevent them from remembering the assault. Drugs and alcohol can cause diminished capacity, a legal term that varies in definition

12. Multiple Perpetrator/Gang Rape:Occurs when two or more perpetrators act together to sexually assault the same victim. Some common aspects of multiple-perpetrator assault include: planning the assault in advance; using substance-facilitated sexual assault; using the assault to introduce or reinforce membership in a group, such as a gang, sports team, or club; targeting a victim that has an existing connection with one of the perpetrators, often sexual in nature; beginning as a consensual activity and introducing others to participate against the victim's will or without consent

13. Sexual Harassment: Is unwanted and unwelcome sexual behavior that interferes with your life, work, or education. This behavior can include verbal or physical acts as well as acts that affect you by creating an environment that is "hostile." The harassment can take place in many different contexts: on the streets, on public transportation, in public places, or in schools, workplaces, institutions, and so on. Sexual harassment can include actions such as sexual comments, physical contact such as someone brushing up against you, demands for sexual behavior from someone who is in a position of authority or power over you (for example, a boss or a teacher), and the creation of a hostile environment.

14. Date Rape: Is a specific kind of acquaintance rape referring to assault(s) experienced by the victim from the person they are on the date with.

Our 2021 report, Sexual Violence in South Asia: Legal and Other Barriers to Justice for Survivors, found the implementation of rape laws remain poor and survivors, particularly those from communities marginalized based on caste, class, and ethnicity, face many obstacles in accessing justice, including:

- corruption amongst law enforcement officials,
- failure of the police to register cases of sexual violence,
- the continued use of the two-finger test,

- difficulties in accessing support services for survivors including compensation and victim and witness protection,
- pressure from families, community and panchayat members to enter into extra-legal settlements and many others.

The punishment for an act of rape- The punishment is rigorous imprisonment of 7 years to life and the person will also be liable to pay a fine.

How is aggravated rape defined under the IPC?

1. Special provisions are provided for cases of aggravated rape under the IPC, as amended by the Criminal Law (Amendment) Act, 2013. A rape is considered aggravated if it meets any of the following conditions:
2. Rape by someone having authority over the woman because of legal status (for example: police officer, army personnel)
3. Rape by someone who is in a position of trust in relation with the survivor (for example: family, hospital staff)
4. Special nature of woman (a pregnant woman, a mentally ill woman, a woman who cannot give consent, a woman below the age of sixteen)
5. Rape involving violent circumstances (rape during time of communal riots, repeatedly raping someone)
6. Other forms of aggravated rape include where the survivor die from the rape, where the survivor ends up in a vegetative state or where the survivor is gang raped.

One of the major gaps in rape laws in India is the failure to criminalize marital rape. Laws which explicitly allow marital rape under the law treat women as the property of their husbands and render them vulnerable to sexual violence and abuse within marriage. The law has a wide definition of rape which includes all acts of sexual penetration, as well as acts of oral sex (without a requirement for penetration). Indian law takes into account a broad range of coercive circumstances. Indian law presumes the absence of consent on the part of the victim in a broad range of circumstances such as rape by an individual in a position of authority, custodial rape, rape by a relative, guardian, teacher, person in a position of trust, or person in a position of control or dominance over a woman. The law specifically provides that the previous sexual experience of the victim is not relevant in sexual violence cases. Indian law also has a specific provision prohibiting the defence from adducing evidence or asking questions in cross-examination relating to the general immoral character, or previous sexual experience, of the victim while proving consent or the quality of such consent.

Equality Now aims to ensure our advocacy and communications are informed by the needs, experiences, and voices of women and children survivors who are of sexual violence and that all of our work is based on accurate information and evidence, as we work to help survivors in India identify the key obstacles they face in accessing justice. This law covers a wide ambit of acts that constitute sexual harassment, including unwanted verbal or physical advances of any kind. This law is not limited by location at which the sexual harassment takes place, unlike the law to prevent sexual harassment at work places which is explained in a later section. The punishment for (i), (ii) and (iii) as given above is rigorous imprisonment for a term that may extend to 3 years, or a fine, or both while the punishment for (iv) is either simple or rigorous imprisonment for a term which may extend to 1 year, or a fine, or both. Section 354B of the IPC criminalises assault or use of criminal force against a woman with the intention of disrobing her, i.e. with the intention of depriving her of her clothing or forcing her to be naked. Such an act is punishable with either simple or rigorous imprisonment of 3 to 7 years and a fine. Aiding such a crime also carries the same punishment. While this may sound similar to outraging modesty, it isn't. It is considered an offence whether or not the man intended to outrage the modesty of the woman. In case of Rape- A person accused of aggravated rape can be imprisoned from ten

years to life along with a fine.In case of gang rape or one where during the act of rape, the accused kills the woman or puts in her in a persistent vegetative state, he can be charged with 20 years rigorous imprisonment to life, or be given a death sentence. The Supreme Court has defined persistent vegetative state as a state where the victim is alive but not aware of her environment.

9
WOMEN IN EMPLOYMENT -SITUATION AT WORK PLACE

Every work of art is the child of its time;
often it is the mother of our emotions.

<u>Vassily Kandinsky</u>

India is a traditional country and there is diversity in religions, culture, and customs. The role of the women in India mostly is household and limited to domestic issues. In some cases, women can find employment as nurses, doctors, teachers in the caring and nurturing sectors. But even if well-qualified women engineers or managers or geologists are available, preference will be given to a male of equal qualification. In the history of human development, women have been as vital in history-making as men have been. In fact, higher status for women vis-à-vis employment and work performed by them in a society is a significant indicator of a nation's overall progress. There are many reasons and problems that forced Indian women to work. The financial demands on Indian families are increasing day by day. Cost of living, expenses on the education of children, and cost of housing properties in India raised, and these reasons force every family in India to look for ways and means of increasing the household income. As a result, women in India who were mostly known as homemakers are forced to go for jobs and take up even careers that were considered only suitable for men such as working in night shifts.

Working women i.e., those who are in paid employment, face problems at the workplace just by virtue of their being women. Social attitude to the role of women lags much behind the law. The attitude which considers women fit for certain jobs and not others causes prejudice in those who recruit employees. Thus women find employment easily as nurses, doctors, teachers, secretaries, or on the assembly line. Even when well-qualified women are available, preference is given to a male candidate of equal qualifications. A gender bias creates an obstacle at the recruitment stage itself. When it comes to remuneration, though the law proclaims equality, it is not always practiced. The inbuilt conviction that women are incapable of handling arduous jobs and are less efficient than men influences the payment of unequal salaries and wages for the same job. But in most families, her salary is handed over to the father, husband, or in-laws. So the basic motive for seeking employment in order to gain economic independence is nullified in many women's cases. Problems of gender bias beset women in the industrial sector when technological advancement results in the retrenchment of employees.

"No nation can ever be worthy of its existence that cannot take its women along with the men. No struggle can ever succeed without women participating side by side with men. There are two powers in the world; one is the sword and the other is the pen. There is a great competition and rivalry between the two. There is a third power stronger than both, that of the women."— Muhammad Ali Jinnah, founder of Pakistan

In India mostly it is women who have to do household as cooking, cleaning the house, doing the dishes, washing clothes, care of children and men do not share most of the household works. Men do that work that is to be dealt with outside the house. Now a day there is an increasing need for getting some income for the family then women have to work harder. Women workers have to handle Persecution at their workplace, sometimes just overlook things to ensure that their job is not jeopardized in any way. Many Indian families are still living as joint families along with their parents and in-laws. This adds to their stress further because they have to please all the family members of her husband. Listen to their complaints that they make against her and turn deaf ears towards them and so on. Overall, the majority of women in India look towards or live in the hope that things will change.

Most women in India work and contribute to the economy in one form or another, much of their work is not documented or accounted for in official statistics. Women plow fields and harvest crops while working on farms, women weave and make handicrafts while working in household industries, women sell food and gather wood while working in the informal sector. Additionally, women are traditionally responsible for the daily household chores (e.g., cooking, fetching water, and looking after children). Although the cultural restrictions women face are changing, women are still not as free as men to participate in the formal economy. In the past, cultural restrictions were the primary impediments to female employment now, however; the shortage of jobs throughout the country contributes to low female employment as well. The Indian census divides workers into two categories: "main" and "marginal" workers. Main workers include people who worked for 6 months or more during the year, while marginal workers include those who worked for a shorter period. Many of these workers are agricultural laborers. Unpaid farm and family enterprise workers are supposed to be included in either the main worker or marginal worker category, as appropriate. Women account for a small proportion of the formal Indian labor force, even though the number of female main workers has grown faster in recent years than that of their male counterparts.

Dr. B.R. Ambedkar made a lot of excellent and necessary actions towards Indian women at the time. Thanks to our constitution and the struggles of Indian women, Indian women have won respect in society. So, they are treated equally with men in all facets of life. The constitution guarantees women's equality and empowers the nation to take positive initiatives in their favor.

Factors affecting the employment of women

Numerous barriers work against women's access to employment, economic empowerment and socio-economic fortunes. Education is a very critical factor in advancing women's employment and socio-economic involvement. The various socio-economic factors are mentioned below:

1) Social Behaviour is the most important factor, and it is also the most accountable for female unemployment. This mentality, which prevents women from seeking employment, stems from a long-standing cultural tradition. It made them remain home and care for the family. Women's work is largely constrained by social attitude and perception. (Women working outside the home are unsuitable, undesirable, and potentially damaging to their chastity and femininity virtues.)

2) Families still believe that daughters should not be permitted to earn an income. If they are allowed to work, their wages will not

be utilized to maintain the family. Fathers are reluctant to let their daughters work and to use their money to help pay for household expenses. Girls are usually discouraged from leaving town for school or work (Again economic compulsions are weakening such traditions and customs but not enough to mend them). Women are either forbidden from obtaining jobs or are legally prohibited from doing so. For instance, in India, women are not allowed to drive taxis, trucks, or cars due to safety concerns. Women are involved in society, but not in construction.

3) In modern society, marriage has a negative impact on a woman's ability to find work. Therefore, she enters the job market late or returns to the market after a period of time because they have occasionally had to leave their jobs due to marriage. For females, this particular custom takes precedence over everything else, and marriage is the first priority in their lives as a consequence of which they leave their jobs and face the difficulty of re-entry and otherwise late entry into the labor market as a result.

4) Female domestic responsibilities have been women's primary responsibilities since ancient times, as though they were created for this purpose. It has a negative impact on one's employment prospects. They are only required to perform those tasks that will allow them to devote sufficient time to household responsibilities. Women attempt to avoid job assignments that interfere with their household activities and schedule, which can have a negative impact on their opportunities for advancement and employment.

5) Workers' employment is hindered by a lack of mobility, which might be caused by domestic tasks or inadequacy in child care arrangements. While occupational diversity and mobility are not particularly tough propositions for males, they are extremely difficult propositions for women. Women are unable to simply relocate due to family obligations and a lack of professional skills. When males leave, however, all of the family obligations fall on the shoulders of the women. Women are physically and mentally immobile in terms of location, time, and energy. Likewise, their movement in terms of time is restricted throughout pregnancy and

for the first few months following the birth of the child.

6) Indian society has a long-standing tradition of entrusting female children with the responsibility of caring for their younger siblings, whether partially or fully. Female children are often asked to care for their younger siblings even when they are still children themselves. The responsibility of bearing and raising kids forces people to make compromises in their professional lives.

7) The way female children are raised in our society, particularly in rural and small-town settings, leads to their becoming reliant on males. Even as adults, females rely on a male member of their family to accompany them on their travels. It forces people to remain limited to their current location, so limiting their employment choices and options for advancement.

8) In terms of safety and security, women who accept jobs outside of their hometown confront the challenge of finding safe and secure housing. Many employed people who have transferable jobs find it extremely difficult to relocate because they are concerned that they will not be able to find suitable housing in their new location. As a result, women attempt to escape this predicament at the expense of their employment, and there are only a limited number of working women's hostels available. They like to work in their local area if it is an option. It becomes an obstacle to women's ability to obtain a gainful job.

9) For the obvious fact that when boys marry, they eventually become the principal breadwinners in their own families, Indians continue to place a higher value on their education and occupations than those of girls. In Indian society, investing in male children's education takes precedence over other investments. Female children are rarely given preference when it comes to educational opportunities, particularly at the higher level.

10) job-oriented courses of a fundamental kind are often favored by females over males in terms of training. A huge number of women are enrolled in technical colleges, boutique & fabric painting, and other such elementary courses that prepare them for low-wage positions in the secondary labor market. Female career

advancement is therefore often restricted as a result of this. Especially in the business sector, there aren't many programs that are specifically designed for women.

11) Women are less likely than men to be unionized because they have a double burden of duty. Women workers are particularly vulnerable due to a lack of unionization, which does not motivate them to struggle against sex-based issues such as discrimination in promotion & training courses. As a consequence, discrimination against women in India was unable to be completely eliminated.

12) The belief that women are not the major breadwinners in their families and that they merely offer supplemental income has resulted in widespread exploitation of women. Women have been relegated to lower-level positions as a result of the poor wages they receive. Women teachers in small towns and cities are paid less than the min wage that is paid to male employees in these areas. Wage discrimination discourages people from focusing on their performance, and as a result, their career advancement is stymied.

13) Women who work as a supplement to their family's income do so when the family's economic situation requires it or warrants it, and they leave when the family's financial situation allows it. Women work when their families are experiencing financial difficulties; they are requested to provide a helping hand to ensure the family's survival. Women work solely for the benefit of their families, instead of for their personal benefit and sustenance. Females enter the labor force when men's earnings become inconsistent, inadequate, or withheld from them. Women's ability to be flexible in the labor market is limited by the option of recruitment exercised by the family.

14) Gender-Based Discrimination Labour: The division of labor based on gender, which has spread beyond household duties to work full time in recent years. In agriculture, women are primarily engaged in labor-intensive jobs that are physically demanding, repetitive, and low-paying in nature. The division of labor on the basis of gender can be observed even in industries where women are employed in significant numbers, such as textiles, export-

oriented industries such as apparel, electronics, and the building and construction industries. Despite the fact that India has a huge number of labor regulations, these rules tend to neglect the experiences of women and have a paternalistic outlook on life.

15) Social Security Measures for Women: Social security is a crucial requirement for all women, regardless of the type of employment in which they are employed and the hours that they work. When it comes to employment, women are subjected to a variety of variables, including sickness, maternity, disability, job uncertainties, and hazards. Through the improvement of working and living conditions as well as the provision of women with security against the uncertainty of the future, they contribute significantly to the realization of the welfare state goal.

Sexual Harassment of Women At Workplace

Sexual Harassment is behavior. It is defined as unwelcome behavior of sexual nature. Sexual harassment at the workplace is a widespread problem in the world whether it be a developed nation or a developing nation or an underdeveloped nation, atrocities against women are common everywhere. It is a universal problem giving a negative impact on both men and women. It is happening more with women's gender in particular. How much ever one tries to protect, prohibit, prevent and give remedies such violation will always take place. It is a crime against women, who are considered to be the most vulnerable section of society. That is why they have to suffer all these immunes starting from female feticide, human trafficking, stalking, sexual abuse, sexual harassment, to the most heinous crime Rape. It is unlawful to harass a person (an applicant or an employee) because of that person's sex.Harassment can include "sexual harassment" or unwelcome sexual advances, requests for sexual favors, and other verbal or physical harassment of a sexual nature. Sexual Harassment is unwelcome sexual behavior, which could be expected to meet a person feel offended, humiliated or intimated. It can be physical, verbal and written.Unwelcome Behavior is the critical word. Unwelcome does not mean "involuntary." A victim may consent or agree to certain conduct and actively participate in it even though it is offensive and objectionable. Therefore, sexual conduct is unwelcome whenever the person subjected to it considers it unwelcome. Whether the person in fact welcomed a request for a date, sex-oriented comment, or joke depends on all the circumstances.

Provisions for women

Sexual misbehavior is a form of violence in which another person is harmed by the use of power, control, and/or intimidation. Sexual assault, sexual abuse, domestic abuse, dating violence, & stalking all fall under this category. It occurs when consent is not given. Consent is a freely offered and unambiguous consent, not the absence of a no, and it cannot be obtained if a person is intoxicated or under the influence of drugs. Sexual misconduct is viewed as a breach of fundamental freedom and justice as well as a discriminating issue affecting health and safety. It is fundamentally insulting and threatens the rights of women to equality of opportunity and treatment at work. The most important approach should be to avoid such harassment; but, if it does occur, it should be punished as well as the victim should be well protected.

The provisions for women are described as follows:

1. The Maternity Benefit Act was enacted to reduce disparities and introduce standardization to the rates, qualification conditions, & length of maternity benefits. The Act also completely negates the Mines Maternity Benefit Act, the Bombay Maternity Benefit Act, the Plantation Labour Act, and any other provincial enactments on the same issue.

2. The Workmen's Compensation Act is a federal law that provides for the compensation of injured workers. Specifically, it deals with matters where an accident or disease happens at the workplace, resulting in the death or handicap of women workers. This includes financial losses as well as the loss of housekeeping duties. In the event of death, the amount of

compensation is equivalent to 50 % of the monthly income or an amount equal to Rs 80,000, whichever is higher, as compensation. However, the legislation that applies to women workers will be the primary focus of our discussion.

3. The Minimum Wages Act is largely intended to protect employees in the developing world, which accounts for the vast bulk of women's employment. Its purpose is to provide statutory minimum wages for scheduled employments in order to reduce the likelihood of labour being exploited through the payment of very cheap and sweaty wages, among other things. It also defines the minimum regular working time, the weekly rest day, and the possibility of overtime.

This Act was passed to govern the salaries and wages to people employed in industry and provide them with a swift and efficient remedy in the event of illegal deductions from their salaries or unjustifiable delays in the payment of their wages. In the context of wages, any sums of money or benefits payable to an employee include, but are not limited to, any sums due upon leaving the service, wages in replacement of vacations or leave, overtime earnings, and any bonuses due. (This does not include the value of any dwelling accommodations, the provision of light, drinking, medical care, contributions to any pension plans, travel, or any other expenses.)

- Auxiliary Principles of State Policy, Part IV of the Equal Remuneration Act. For example, Article 39 of the Constitution mandates that the state lead policy and those employers pay the same compensation to men and women who perform the same or similar work. The Law now covers almost every sort of facility, a considerable expansion. Even if the work is being done in separate locations, the compensation must be the same. If the employment of women is outlawed or restricted by law, a company is not permitted to discriminate against them when recruiting new employees. As a result, employers are forbidden from sex discrimination in things like recruiting, promotion, training, and transfer.

Unemployment and temporary work are more common among women than among men. Most women workers do not have any social security or access to health care benefits. As a result, work-related illnesses, like mental pressure and other health problems, remain hidden. As per available research, a large number of women workers complain of frequent headaches, back pain, circulatory disorders, fatigue, and emotional and mental disorders resulting from performing various activities at the workplace. Around the world, finding a job is much tougher for women than it is for men. When women are employed, they tend to work in low-quality jobs in vulnerable conditions, and there is little improvement forecast in the near future. The relationship between female labor force participation and development is complex, including changes in economic growth, education, fertility rates, social standards, and other factors. However, women's labor participation rates only tell part of the story. Understanding women's employment is crucial. Policies should target both labor demand and supply to improve job quality. Expanding secondary school education is important, but so is creating jobs that women can access. One of the most important things would be that the women who are dealing with the issue of women's rights and advantages in India are doing so in a positive way. From ancient times to the present day, women have struggled to achieve social prestige and a respected position in society. At the time, Women in India were in desperate need of laws to enhance their social standing and to ensure sufficient protection against physical and mental torture.

A safe workplace with equitable treatment irrespective of one's sex, caste, creed, religion, or socio-economic background is the basic right any person is entitled to through the Indian Constitution. But asK. Lakshmi Raghuramaiah, President of The All-India Women's Conference said, ***"'Discrimination,' 'exploitation,' and 'suppression' are no words to be*** *used as weapons in the battle of sexes. Work is the right of everyone. Women have the right and duty to organize themselves for better protection and work together with peace, justice, and equality for the progress of the nation. When we do this, we do not need International Women's Years, decades, demonstrations and processions,"*

10

DOWRY—CAUSE FOR INJUSTICE FROM WOMB TO TOMB

Start marrying a woman for love and stop divorcing a woman for money.

The ancient custom of dowry, that is, bride-to-groom transfers at the time of marriage, remains ubiquitous in several countries. In this article we focus on rural India, where dowry remains a widespread phenomenon despite being illegal since 19611—according to the 2006 Rural Economic and Demographic Survey (REDS), dowry was paid in 95 percent of marriages during 1960-2008. Dowry per marriage often amounts to several years of household income and imposes a substantial burden on girls' families. However, little is known about the evolution of dowry in recent decades that have witnessed remarkable economic and social change.

Dowry, commonly known as 'dahej' includes any gift that is not offered by the bride's side on their own and anything that the groom's side asks for, directly or indirectly. The groom's side must compel the bride's side to fulfill their demands. If the groom's side makes any demand as a precondition to marriage, without which the bride's side anticipates that the marriage might be called off, then also such demand will be considered as dowry.Dowry means any property or valuable security given or agreed to be given either directly or indirectly:

1. by one party to a marriage to the other party to the marriage; or
2. by the parents of either party to a marriage or by any other person, to either party to the marriage or to any other person; at or before or any time after the marriage in connection with the marriage of said parties but does not include dower or Mahr in the case of persons to whom the Muslim Personal Law (Shariat) applies.

Any young man, who makes dowry a condition to marriage, discredits his education and his country and dishonors womanhood.-Mahatma Gandhi

Even in the oldest available records, such as the Code of Hammurabi, the dowry is described as an already-existing custom.

Regulations surrounding the custom include: the wife being entitled to her dowry at her husband's death as part of her dower, her dowry being inheritable only by her own children, not by her husband's children by other women, and a woman not being entitled to a (subsequent) inheritance if her father had provided her dowry in marriage. If a woman died without sons, her husband had to refund the dowry but could deduct the value of the bride price; the dowry would normally have been the larger of the sums. One of the basic functions of a dowry has been to serve as a form of protection for the wife against the possibility of ill-treatment by her husband and his family. In other words, the dowry provides an incentive to the husband not to harm his wife.

The Dowry system in Indian Marriages can be called the commercial aspect of marriage. The practice of giving dowry was very common among all people of all nations. A girl gets all the domestic utensils that are necessary to set up a family. The Dowry system in India was prevalent since the Vedic period. In the Epic period gifts from parents, brothers and relatives, and relatives were recognized as women's property-stridhan. According to Kautilya —Means of subsistence or jewelry constitute what is called the use of the property of the woman. It is no guilt for a wife to make use of this property in maintaining her son her daughter-in-law or herself if her absent husband has made no provision for her maintenance. Since British rule to date, efforts are being put to root out one draconian evil from Indian society which is the dowry system but in spite of huge efforts cornered, evil persists in all aspects everywhere in the country. The problem is no more confined to one or two states or north Indian states but gained roots in the soil of Southern as well as Eastern states too. The problematic part is that it made its way to all sections, classes, castes, societies, and communities. It permitted even to tribal societies known for primitive egalitarianism and gender equality and to Muslim community too. Strong legislation, laws, and women's movements, every attempt to resist it has been thwarted by the wide social sanction accorded to this illegal practice

In India, it has its roots in medieval times when a gift in cash or kind was given to a bride by her family to maintain her independence after marriage. During the colonial period, it became the only legal way to get married, with the British making the practice of dowry mandatory. In India Dowry was regally designed to safeguard the women and it was considered to be Streedhan which means a wealth of a woman in form of money,gift, property given solely to the woman by her parents at the time of marriage. The abuse of this custom eroded and aborted the original meaningful function of dowry as a safety net for the woman and was corrupted to become the price tag for the groom and consequently the noose for the bride.

Dowry is the money, goods, or the estate that the bride's family gives to the groom's family at the time of the wedding. This practice is common in cultures that are strongly patrilineal, patrilocal, and have male-biased inheritance laws. Dowry payments in India's villages have been largely stable over the past few decades, a World Bank study has found. Researchers looked at 40,000 marriages that took place in rural India between 1960 and 2008. They found that dowry was paid in 95% of the marriages even though it's been illegal in India since 1961. The practice, often described as a social evil, continues to thrive and leaves women vulnerable to domestic violence and even death. Paying and accepting dowry is a centuries-old tradition in South Asia where the bride's parents gift cash, clothes, and jewelry to the groom's family. The study was based on dowry data from 17 Indian states that contain 96% of India's population. It focussed on rural India since a majority of Indians continue to live in villages.

These days, the word 'gift' is sometimes used as a euphemism instead of 'dowry'. Families that like to pose as progressive might use the word 'gift' to disassociate themselves from the act of giving or receiving dowry. However, even when dressed up in the polite and fancy term of a "gift", it still remains dowry, something which is illegal. Dowry is also most often defined and perceived as a payment made at the time of the marriage. But it is worth noting that there is a continuous nature to the payment of dowry which is often ignored. The cash and goods paid do not stop at one event i.e. the marriage. Mostly, the bride's family is expected to make recurring payments through the life of the couple's alliance on festivals, special occasions like the birth of a son, etc. These payments are made because they are the norm and non-payment of these payments can warrant humiliation and harassment of the bride in the groom's family. The recurring nature of dowry is still not an extensive part of academic literature and research. It continues to be restricted to the payment made at the time of the marriage only.

In India, marriage continues to be the ultimate goal notwithstanding academic or professional achievements. A woman choosing to not marry or marry late would most likely be disparaged and ostracized. Since marriage is so important in Indian society and even more so for women, parents are always engrossed in finding a "good groom" for their daughters and are also willing to pay large dowries to secure the said "good groom". In the Indian marriage market, the groom occupies a dominant position. Dowries continue to be demanded and the bride's parents have no option but to try to meet the demands. Wealthy households disguise a criminal offense—the act of giving and receiving dowry by opulent weddings and ugly displays of riches. On the contrary, women from middle-class and poor households continue to be harassed, humiliated, assaulted, and killed for not meeting the dowry demands.

Types of dowry crime in India

- Cruelty-cruelty in the form of harassment or torturing the women. The cruelty could be in the form of verbal attack or may be accompanied by beating or harassment in order to force the woman or her family to yield to dowry demand.
- Domestic violence-It includes a broad spectrum of abusive and threatening behavior which include physical, emotional harassment.
- Abetment to suicide-Continuing abuse by her husband and his family members with threats to harm could lead to women

committing suicide . The offense of abetment to suicide is significant because in many cases, the accused persons often bring up a defense that the victim committed suicide of her own volition, even though this may not be true in reality.

- Dowry death-Most dowry deaths occur when the young woman, unable to bear the harassment and torture, commits suicide by hanging herself or consuming poison. Dowry deaths also include bride burning where brides are doused in kerosene and set ablaze by the husband or his family. Sometimes, due to their abetment to commit suicide, the bride may end up setting herself on fire.

Dowry is not the only problem of Indian society, attached to it is the whole bunch of corresponding evils. International women's conferences in Australia accepted that female feticide is directly related to dowry. Middle and lower-middle-income groups who are not able to fulfill the demand of dowry think it wise to nip in the bud. Domestic violence is another consequence of this evil. This colossal problem persists even after centuries, is mainly because stringent laws alone cannot bring change at the level of the mentality of people for that mass movement needs to be initiated. Mass awareness is to be created. Hundreds of dowry deaths are closed as just kitchen accidents or suicides. Around 40 percent of women married happen to be below eighteen years of age and illiterate thus not in a position to assert themselves. Their voice remains unheard in society.

Marriage is considered as a process whereby the responsibility of safety, good life and care provided by father to daughter is passed on to the husband for a very high dowry price. The dowry price of a groom is staggeringly high in Indian society irrespective of class and caste structure and to some extent even the religion, that generations may have to toil to repay the debts incurred during marriages. Many times they are never able to come out of the debt. However, this also does not give a sure-shot guarantee of the lifelong happiness and safety of their daughters and they are either brutally killed or commit suicide due to torture.

According to an Asian proverb 'bringing up a daughter is like watering the neighbor's garden'.

Reforms and laws

Thereafter, various reforms were enforced to remove women's age-old and tradition-ridden handicaps. Some of the Acts thus legislated were the Sati Abolition Act, 1829, the Hindu Widow's re-marriage Act, 1856, the Immoral Traffic Act of 1923, the Child Marriage Restraint Act, 1937. These measures helped considerably in restoring women from total degradation in the social structure.

That was not all. The post-Independence legislation, ensuing from the constitution, proclaimed the fundamental right of women to economic, political and legal equality.......affirmed the right of full and equal franchise for all adults ... directed the State to endeavor to provide free and compulsory education for all children until they completed the age of fourteen.

The Special Marriage Act of 1954, allowed marriage irrespective of religious affiliations. Divorce by mutual consent was permitted. The Hindu Marriage Act, of 1955 made monogamy the rule for both men and women. This Act provided for the registration of marriage. Divorce became permissible under certain conditions. The petition for divorce could be presented by either the husband or the wife. The mother has conferred the custody of children up to the age of five but the guardianship rested with the father. The age of marriage was fixed at the minimum of 15 for girls and 18 for boys. The Hindu Succession and Adoption and Maintenance Act, of 1956 conferred equal rights of inheritance to the father's property to the Hindu daughter and the son, and one-fourth in the case of the coparcenary. Similarly, a widow got an equal footing with the son and daughter to her husband's property. The woman is now empowered to adopt children if she is a widow, a spinster, or a divorcee, or if her husband has become an ascetic or apostate or has been declared of unsound mind by a competent court. Consent of the wife is necessary if a man wishes to adopt. Earlier, a woman was not legally competent to make an adoption, nor was her consent required if her husband made an adoption. A widow could adopt only with the authority and direction left by her deceased husband. The right of a mother to be the guardian of her minor child was recognized but this could be defeated by any testamentary appointment made by her husband. A mother could not appoint a guardian for her children by will.

The Hindu Minority and Guardianship Act, 1956, entitled a wife to maintenance for life. Children both legitimate and illegitimate were entitled to be maintained by parents.

The Dowry Prohibition Act, of 1961 consolidated the anti-dowry laws which had been passed on certain states. This legislation provides for a penalty in section 3 if any person gives, takes, or abets giving or receiving of dowry. The punishment could be imprisonment for a minimum of 5 years and a fine of more than 15,000 or the value of the dowry received, whichever is higher. Dowry in the Act is defined as any property or valuable security given or agreed to be given in connection with the marriage. The penalty for giving or taking dowry is not applicable in the case of presents that are given at the time of marriage without any demand having been made.

The Act provides the penalty for directly or indirectly demanding dowry and provides for a penalty involving a prison term of not less than 6 months and extendable up to two years along with a fine of 10,000. Dowry agreements are void ab initio and if any dowry is received by anyone other than the woman, it should be transferred to the woman. The burden of proving that an offense was not committed is on the persons charged and not on the victim or her family. Under its powers to frame rules for carrying out its objectives under the Act, the government of India has framed the Maintenance of Lists of Presents to the Bride and the Bridegroom Rules, 1985. There are also several state-level amendments to the Dowry Prohibition Act.

All these Acts were passed to give women equal rights in marriage, divorce, inheritance, adoption and to make the demand for dowry an offense. There is, however, no uniform Civil Code because these reformist laws apply so far to Hindus, Buddhists, Jains, and Sikhs and not to Muslims, Christians, and Parsees, who are still governed by their religious laws, constituting what amounts to lacuna for the concerned sections of women.

Misuse of Anti-Dowry Law-Misuse of anti-dowry law to blackmail husbands has become a common practice. The number of false 498A cases or cases of misuse of anti-dowry laws has even made the Supreme Court of India term it as 'legal terrorism. The biased nature of this law has enabled women to file a false case against their husbands for reasons such as:

- To get out of the marriage due to her inability to adjust to the new family.
- Blackmailing the husband to extort money.
- To implicate the husband in a false case and rekindle with a man she was previously associated with or got into an extra-marital affair with.

A lot has changed in India between 2008 and now. But researchers say the trends or patterns of dowry payments were not likely to be too different today in the absence of any "dramatic changes or structural breaks in marriage markets, laws, the human capital of men and women and women's labor market outcomes". In India, marriage decisions are largely taken by the family of the bride. The families look for a groom from within the same religion, the same caste, and also from the same economic status. Marriage outside of caste and religion is very rare and unpopular. Matrimonial apps catering to specific religions and castes have also infiltrated modern dating. Dowry is considered the major contributor to observed violence against women in India. Dowry is a social evil that caused unimaginable tortures and crimes towards women. There are a lot of cases of dowry death which we hear for decades. In all such cases, we hear how the in-laws, husband, and family members torture the woman which

results from either suicide or in some cases she gets killed by them. Lack of political participation due to social-economic constraints is another reason why the woman has not been able to assert herself and protect against this evil. This is also considered the failure of male-oriented polity by some experts. Due to all these disadvantageous positions of women, we fail to solve this problem even after all attention and focus on it. Women's education and enhanced participation in the political process, position in decision-making bodies will improve the situation. They need to be provided with the shield of protection which should not be blunt like present laws but Dowry originated in upper caste families as the wedding gift to the bride from her family. The dowry was later given to help with marriage expenses and became a form of insurance in the case that her in-laws mistreated her. Although the dowry was legally prohibited in 1961, it continues to be highly institutionalized.

11

WOMEN AND ALCOHOLISM— UNENDING AGONY AND ANGUISH

Many persons have a wrong idea of what constitutes true happiness. It is not attained through self-gratification, but through fidelity to a
worthy purpose.

<u>Helen Keller</u>

This chapter discuss the two major sides due to which women bear immense physical torture, social disrespect, and innumerable economic misery, is the problem of alcoholism by their spouses and speaks the suffering of women due to this particular problem and provides suggestions too. Interestingly the chapter also covers the other side of the coin which is the increasing trend of alcohol consumption by women in the current time and its adverse impact on their lives and health.

Domestic violence is deeply rooted in gender-based norms, socialization practices, structural factors and policies that discriminate against women and which underlie and endorse or ignore men's abusive practices against women. It is a widely-held belief that alcohol contributes to disinhibition, mood enhancement, and alcohol myopia in men. Specifically, with respect to intimate partner violence, alcohol disinhibits men from engaging in restraint in contexts in which it is socially and culturally acceptable to engage in verbal or physical abuse against their spouse as well as to exhibit risky sexual behaviors such as inconsistent condom use and having multiple extramarital sexual partners. Indirectly, as a mood enhancer, alcohol can also increase existing feelings of anger and frustration.

Alcohol abuse and alcoholism within a family is a problems that can destroy a marriage or drive a wedge between members. That means people who drink can blow through the family budget, cause fights, ignore children, and otherwise impair the health and happiness of the people they love. In time, family members may even develop symptoms of codependency, inadvertently keeping the addiction alive, even though it harms them. Family therapy and rehab can help.

Alcohol Causes Marital Issues & Ruins Relationships

As the National Council on Alcoholism and Drug Dependence discusses, the following are some of the ways in which problem drinking affects family members, employers, colleagues, fellow students, and others:

1. Neglect of important duties: Alcohol impairs one's cognitive functions and physical capabilities, and this, at some point, will likely result in neglect of responsibilities associated with work, home life, and/or school.

2. Needing time to nurse hangovers: Alcohol has various short-term side effects, such as hangovers. The physical state of a hangover may be temporary, but it can significantly disrupt a person's ability to meet commitments as well as invite unhealthy behaviors, such as poor eating and a lack of exercise.

3. Encountering legal problems: Drinking can increase a person's likelihood of getting into fights, displaying disorderly conduct in

public, driving under the influence, and becoming involved in domestic disputes or violence.

4. The inability to stop at will: Alcohol is an addictive substance and can lead to physical dependence. Although a person who is physically dependent (i.e., has an increased tolerance among other side effects) is not necessarily addicted, ongoing drinking is a slippery slope that can lead to addiction.

Alcohol and Marital Troubles

Alcohol abuse is a large stressor within a family, whether the person drinking is a parent, child, extended family member, or an older adult like a grandparent. Spouses are uniquely dependent on one another, so if one spouse is abusing alcohol, the other is likely to feel the associated problems. By law, spouses are seen as a financial unit (but not in all instances; for example, a spouse is not usually financially liable for the other spouse's student loan debt). In terms of religion, if the spouses observe one, they have made a vow to unconditionally support one another. When drinking causes a financial drain and/or leads to health issues, problems can flare up and threaten the very bedrock of the relationship. According to the National Institute on Alcohol Abuse and Alcoholism, the following are some of the most common problems that arise between spouses when one partner abuses alcohol:

1. **Marital conflict**
2. **Infidelity**
3. **Domestic violence**
4. **Unplanned pregnancy**
5. **Financial instability**
6. **Stress**
7. **Jealousy**
8. **Divorce**

Regarding financial instability, the earlier discussion on the real and potential economic losses associated with alcohol abuse, as well as debt, can easily trigger profound problems in a marriage. A spouse's alcohol abuse can also trigger a host of emotions, such as feelings of abandonment, unworthiness, guilt, and self-blame. These emotions can all collect into a disorder known as codependency. People may develop a maladjustment to a loved one's drinking that causes them to enable it through the process of caring for it. Individuals who abuse alcohol experience physical impairments that can draw others into caring for them. While some individuals may be able to resist the urge to help, many will not, especially spouses, children, and other family members or concerned individuals in the person's immediate environment.

Over time, the caregiver can habituate to this rescuer and provider role, and even develop an identity based on it. Further, the caregiver grows accustomed to a relationship with the person abusing alcohol that is primarily based on caregiving. The line between helping an alcohol abuser becomes blurred with enabling the alcohol abuser to maintain the addiction. For this reason, literature on codependency used to refer to the caregiving person as a "co-alcoholic."

As with alcohol abuse, treatment for codependence is available and has been proven effective. One of the main goals of codependency treatment is to help realign caregivers with their own needs so they can live personally fulfilling lives, rather than being in constant service to a loved one's addiction.

As a result, the time, effort, and resources formerly dedicated to life-sustaining activities, such as working and spending time with the family, are disrupted. Initially, a person may think that abusing alcohol will help them deal with these stressors, but as they continue to drink a lot, over time, this abuse can turn into dependence on the substance. Once individuals become psychologically addicted, alcohol abuse can become all-consuming. As individuals are often part of social networks, it is easy to understand how alcohol abuse has a ripple effect across a person's entire network of family, friends, employers, colleagues, and anyone else who depends on the person.

Alcohol, when it is consumed in large quantities for a long period has its impact on the body of the individual who consumes it. It causes various damages to organs, most of them irreversible. The diseases alcoholism causes are many and most of them are terminal in nature. It affects the human mind also and as a consequence of this, it prevents a person from performing as a normal human being. It affects his performance in such a way that an alcoholic becomes totally undependable. As alcohol has a mood-altering effect, it makes an alcoholic totally unpredictable and very often violent. As his priority is for his drinks, many of the pressing needs of life get less priority, and usually, it is the care required for the members of the family that loses its importance in the personal agenda of an alcoholic.

Alcoholism has destroyed many families and the family life of many individuals. This has to be given a lot of importance, as a family is the smallest unit of society. Coherence and love are very essential to bind a family together. Alcohol Problems in the Family records, "Alcohol problems in families are important because families are important. The essential functions of the family are to meet the needs of its members for physical, psychological, social, and economic security and well-being, and the provision of a satisfactory environment for the support, education, and socialization of children. All of these functions can be jeopardized by the problematic consumption of alcohol.

When one thinks of alcoholism usually the alcoholic and his problems come to the mind. What is often forgotten is the indirect victims, especially the family members. Derek Rutherford in his address "Alcohol Problems in the I'luiiily" stales, "Ixss lias can written on the 'forgotten violinist members of the problem drinker's family, both spouses and children. Families of problem drinkers are families in distress. They are 'fragile families' who need help".

Research shows that alcohol use and misuse among women are increasing. While alcohol misuse by anyone presents serious public health concerns, women who drink have a higher risk of certain alcohol-related problems compared to men. To make informed decisions about alcohol use, it is important that women be aware of these health risks and of the Dietary Guidelines for Americans, 2020–2025 for adult women of legal drinking age—they can choose not to drink or to drink in moderation by limiting intake to 1 drink or less in a day when alcohol is consumed. Drinking less is better for health than drinking more. Some individuals should avoid alcohol completely, such as those who are pregnant or might be pregnant.

"I have taken more out of alcohol than alcohol has taken out of me." — Winston Churchill

Long-Term Health Risks

Alcohol is Associated with other Diseases, Injuries, and Harms

1. Alcohol Use Disorder-Alcohol use disorder (AUD) is a chronic relapsing brain disorder characterized by an impaired ability to stop or control alcohol use despite adverse social, occupational, or health consequences. AUD can range from mild to severe, and

recovery is possible regardless of severity. (To be diagnosed with AUD, a person must meet certain diagnostic criteria outlined in the Diagnostic and Statistical Manual of Mental Disorders, 5th edition.

2. Liver Damage-Women who regularly misuse alcohol are more likely than men who drink the same amount to develop alcoholic hepatitis, a potentially fatal alcohol-related liver condition. This pattern of drinking can also lead to cirrhosis (permanent liver scarring).

3. Heart Disease-Long-term alcohol misuse is a leading cause of heart disease. Women are more susceptible to alcohol-related heart disease than men, even though they may consume less alcohol over their lifetime than men.

4. Brain Damage-Research suggests that alcohol misuse produces brain damage more quickly in women than in men. In addition, a growing body of evidence shows that alcohol can disrupt normal brain development during the adolescent years, and there may be differences in the impact of alcohol on the brains of teen girls and boys who drink. For example, in one study, teen girls who reported binge drinking, but not teen boys who reported binge drinking, showed less brain activity and worse performance on a memory test than peers who drank lightly or abstained.8 Similarly, teenage girls who drank heavily showed a greater reduction in the size of important brain areas involved in memory and decision-making than teenage boys who engaged in heavy drinking. Women also may be more susceptible than men to alcohol-related blackouts, which are gaps in a person's memory for events that occurred while they were intoxicated. These gaps happen when a person drinks enough alcohol to temporarily block the transfer of memories from short-term to long-term storage—known as memory consolidation—in a brain area called the hippocampus.

5. Breast Cancer-There is an association between drinking alcohol and developing breast cancer. Studies demonstrate that women who consume about 1 drink per day have a 5 to 9 percent higher

chance of developing breast cancer than women who do not drink at all. That risk increases for every additional drink they have per day.

6. Alcohol and Pregnancy-Any drinking during pregnancy can be harmful. Prenatal alcohol exposure can cause physical, cognitive, and behavioral problems in children, any of which can be components of fetal alcohol spectrum disorders (FASD).

Although men are more likely to drink alcohol and consume larger amounts, biological differences in body structure and chemistry lead most women to absorb more alcohol and take longer to metabolize it. After drinking the same amount of alcohol, women tend to have higher blood alcohol levels than men, and the immediate effects of alcohol usually occur more quickly and last longer in women than men. These differences make women more susceptible to the long-term negative health effects of alcohol compared with men. Women are increasingly suffering from the ill effects of alcohol, too. National data show that the cirrhosis death rate shot up by 57% among women aged 45-64 from 2000-2015 in the US, compared to 21% among men. And it rose 18% in women aged 25-44, despite decreasing by 10% among their male peers. Adult women's visits to hospital emergency departments for overdosing on alcohol also are rising sharply. And risky drinking patterns are escalating among women in particular.

12

WOMEN AND MENTAL ILLNESS - A NEGLECTED ASPECT

*Let us devote our life to worthwhile
actions and feelings, to great thoughts, real affections, and
enduring undertakings.*

<u>Andre Maurois</u>

Mental disorders can affect women and men differently. Some disorders are more common in women such as depression and anxiety. There are also certain types of disorders that are unique to women. For example, some women may experience symptoms of mental disorders at times of hormone change, such as perinatal depression, premenstrual dysphoric disorder, and perimenopause-related depression. When it comes to other mental disorders such as schizophrenia and bipolar disorder, research has not found differences in the rates at which men and women experience these illnesses. But women may experience these illnesses differently – certain symptoms may be more common in women than in men, and the course of the illness can be affected by the sex of the individual. Researchers are only now beginning to tease apart the various biological and psychosocial factors that may impact the mental health of both women and men.Women and men are different not only in their obvious physical attributes, but also in their psychological makeup. There are actual differences in the way women's and men's brains are structured and "wired" and in the way they process information and react to events and stimuli. Women and men differ in the way they communicate, deal in relationships, express their feelings, and react to stress. Thus, the gender differences are based in physical, physiological, and psychological attributes. Women and men can develop most of the same mental disorders and conditions, but may experience different symptoms. Some symptoms include:

1. **Persistent sadness or feelings of hopelessness**
2. **Misuse of alcohol and/or drugs**
3. **Dramatic changes in eating or sleeping habits**
4. **Appetite and/or weight changes**
5. **Decreased energy or fatigue**
6. **Excessive fear or worry**
7. **Seeing or hearing things that are not there**
8. **Extremely high and low moods**
9. **Aches, headaches, or digestive problems without a clear cause**
10. **Irritability**
11. **Social withdrawal**
12. **Suicidal thoughts**

Around one in five women have a common mental health problem such as depression and anxiety. While there can be many reasons why these develop, some risk factors affect many women. Women are more likely than men:

1. to be carers, which can lead to stress, anxiety and isolation.
2. to live in poverty which, along with concerns about personal safety and working mainly in the home, can lead to social isolation
3. to experience physical and sexual abuse, which can have a long-term impact on their mental health. Contact Refuge if you're

experiencing domestic violence
4. to experience sexual violence, which can cause PTSD. We have tips on self-care if you're affected by hearing about sexual violence in the media.

Mental health is a term used to describe either a level of cognitive or emotional well-being or an absence of a mental disorder. From perspectives of the discipline of positive psychology or holism, mental health may include an individual's ability to enjoy life and procure a balance between life activities and efforts to achieve psychological resilience. On the other hand, a mental disorder or mental illness is an involuntary psychological or behavioral pattern that occurs in an individual and is thought to cause distress or disability that is not expected as part of normal development or culture. Gender is a critical determinant of mental health and mental illness. The morbidity associated with mental illness has received substantially more attention than the gender specific determinants and mechanisms that promote and protect mental health and foster resilience to stress and adversity.

"There are wounds that never show on the body that are deeper and more hurtful than anything that bleeds."— Laurell K. Hamilton, Mistral's Kiss

Women's Mental Health Conditions and Symptoms

Every patient—whether male or female, old or young, rich or poor—experiences mental illness in their own unique way. Even though there are similarities in the symptoms and impacts of specific mental health conditions, women often face different challenges than men in how they perceive and experience symptoms, and also in how strategies are devised to treat the disorder.

- Depression-In addition to being more likely than men to experience the disease, some forms of depression are unique to women, as explained by the NIMH. Among the mental disorders tied to changes in women's hormone levels are perinatal depression (depression occurring before and after giving birth, the latter known as postpartum depression), premenstrual dysphoric disorder, and depression related to perimenopause.
- Anxiety-The NIMH defines General Anxiety Disorder (GAD) as experiencing "excessive anxiety or worry" for most days over a period of six months. Other anxiety disorders include panic disorder, obsessive-compulsive disorder, social anxiety disorder (or social phobia), separation anxiety disorder, and phobia-related disorders (such as fear of flying, fear of heights, or fear of specific objects).
- Perinatal depression-WHO estimates that worldwide, 10% of pregnant women and 13% of women who have just given birth experience a mental disorder, primarily depression. Perinatal depression, which encompasses both categories of women, impairs a woman's ability to function and also hinders the development of the child. While pregnant women everywhere are susceptible to perinatal depression and other mental illnesses, the problem is greatest in developing countries, where

WHO estimates that 20% of mothers experience postpartum depression.

- Eating disorders-Twice as many women in the many countries are affected by eating disorders as men: 20 million vs. 10 million, according to figures compiled by the National Eating Disorder Association. The causes of the illnesses remain a mystery for the most part, but researchers believe biology, psychology, and culture are all involved.

- Postpartum depression-This subset of perinatal depression affects some women within one year of giving birth. It is characterized by feelings of extreme sadness, anxiety, and tiredness that impact the woman's ability to care for herself and her baby. The NIMH emphasizes that the condition does not originate with any action on the mother's part, but rather occurs as a result of a combination of physical and emotional factors that include: hormonal changes during pregnancy and after delivering, a lack of sleep in the weeks and months after the baby's arrival, and the physical exhaustion and pain related to pregnancy and giving birth.

- Body dysmorphic disorder-The Cleveland Clinic defines this condition as a person's extreme anxiety about some perceived physical defect. People with body dysmorphic disorder (BDD) constantly seek reassurances about their appearance and may consider themselves "ugly" to the point where they seek a remedy. This remedy may include plastic surgery to remove whatever is considered a physical imperfection.

- Bipolar disorder-This condition, which was previously referred to as "manic-depressive illness," is characterized by wide mood swings that are much more extreme than the ups and downs people normally experience in their day-to-day lives. The drastic changes in mood and energy level can seriously hinder the person's ability to function, particularly for people affected by "bipolar I" (pronounced "bipolar one"), in which the mood swings are more severe than in "bipolar II."

- Borderline personality disorder-NIMH describes borderline personality disorder (BPD) as a mental illness characterized by changeable moods, continually varying self-image, and inconsistent behavior over an extended period of time. According to the Office of Women's Health at HHS, BPD is a "serious mental illness" that causes instability in a person's mood, behavior, relationships, and self-image on a daily basis. While 2% of adults are affected by the disorder, it strikes young women more than any other demographic.

Mental Health: Why the Gender Differences?

In in the female brain and body to differentiate these responses to mental illness-

1. Biological influences. Female hormonal fluctuations are known to play a role in mood and depression. The hormone estrogen can have positive effects on the brain, protecting schizophrenic women from severe symptoms during certain phases of their menstrual cycles and maintaining the structure of neurons in the brain, which protects against some aspects of Alzheimer's. On the less positive side, women tend to produce less of the mood stabilizer serotonin and synthesize it more slowly than men, which may account for the higher rates of depression. A woman's genetic makeup is also believed to play a role in the development of such neurological disorders as Alzheimer's.

2. Socio-cultural influences. Despite strides in gender equality, women still face challenges when it comes to socio-economic power, status, position, and dependence, which can contribute to depression and other disorders. Women are still the primary caregivers for children, and it is estimated that they also provide 80 percent of all caregiving for chronically ill elders, which adds stress to a woman's life. Girls tend to become dissatisfied with their bodies at puberty, a reaction that is linked to depression. Girls are also sexually abused more often than boys, and one in five women will experience rape or attempted rape, which can

lead to depression and panic disorder.

3. Behavioral influences. There is some thinking that women are more apt to report mental health disturbances than men and that doctors are more prone to diagnose a woman with depression and to treat the condition with mood-altering drugs. Women are more likely to report mental health concerns to a general practitioner, while men report tend to discuss them with a mental health specialist. However, women are sometimes afraid to report physical violence and abuse.

Gender differences occur particularly in the rates of common mental disorders (CMDs)-depression, anxiety, and somatic complaints wherein women predominate. Unipolar depression, which is predicted to be the second leading cause of global disability burden by 2020, is twice as common in women. Furthermore, the lifetime risk of anxiety disorders (e.g., generalized anxiety disorder) is 2–3 times higher in females as compared to males. Moreover, depression is not only the most common women's mental health problem, but may be more persistent in women than men.Although depressive symptoms in men and women have generally been found to be similar overall, women are more likely to present with atypical or "reverse vegetative" symptoms such as increased appetite and weight gain. In case of anxiety disorders, females have greater severity of symptoms, have more often comorbid depression and complicated course.

Women's Mental Health Treatment and Resources

Despite the complexity of the mental health challenges women face, treatment options and resources are available to help these women lead healthy lives. Sometimes, the simplest advice is the most effective, and may begin with something as basic as not being afraid to ask for help. Mental health professionals are ready to help women affected by mental illness. They are there to ensure afflicted women receive the treatment and attention they need to start on the road to recovery, and return to health should they ever stray.

For Improving women's mental health

Much of maintaining good mental health entails developing the skills to cope with the ups and downs of everyday life. Some tips and suggestions that teach women of all ages the important coping skills that can prevent small problems from becoming big ones. These are among the helpful tips:

1. Improve your mood by exercising regularly. Aerobic exercise releases endorphins, which are chemicals that help alleviate stress and promote calmness. Regular physical exercise also helps improve sleep habits and quality, and may also reduce the symptoms of anxiety and depression.

2. Eat a balanced diet. Consuming healthy foods has been found to improve people's mood in addition to improving their physical health. In particular, avoid sugary foods, which can lead to tiredness and irritability when blood sugar levels drop. Researchers recommend that alcohol and coffee be consumed in moderation. Also, certain vitamins and minerals—such as selenium, omega-3 fatty acids, folate, vitamin B12, calcium, iron, and zinc—appear to alleviate the symptoms of depression.

3. Find a job you enjoy. Often, a woman's mental health issues can be exacerbated by her employment. A change of job can give such women a renewed sense of purpose and alleviate some of the effects of their illness. However, it can be difficult for women who suffer from mental illness to rejoin the workforce or switch jobs. Many states and mental health services offer vocational rehabilitation services, employment support, and free employment and job counseling services.

One of the greatest challenges facing the health care industry is the fight against mental illness. To begin with, serious conditions such as schizophrenia, bipolar disorder, depression, and anxiety are often difficult to diagnose. But perhaps the most daunting obstacle to treatment of mental health disorders is the societal stigma attached to the diseases. The reluctance of patients to seek treatment for mental health disorders disproportionately affects

women, in large part because women are more susceptible than men to many common mental health conditions. Although severe mental disorders such as schizophrenia and bipolar disorders are less prevalent than CMD, the chronic course and associated disability make these disorders severe. In addition, the stigma associated with these illnesses has a major impact not only on the sufferer but also on the families. Also, the families are burdened with the care of these patients for almost their entire lives in a great number of cases. Needless to say, the emotional and financial strain on the caregivers may be overwhelming.

13
HEALTH CONCERNS OF WOMEN MATTER OF ACCESS AND OUTREACH

Flatter me, and I may not believe you.
Criticize me, and I may not like you.
Ignore me, and I may not forgive you.
Encourage me, and I may not forget you.
- William Arthur Ward

Women's health problems are often misunderstood, and many women don't get the medical attention they need and deserve because there is simply not enough information available to them. To take control of your health, it is important to first understand the various health issues affecting women at various stages of life. Women have unique health issues. And some of the health issues that affect both men and women can affect women differently. Unique issues include pregnancy, menopause, and conditions of the female organs. Women can have a healthy pregnancy by getting early and regular prenatal care. They should also get recommended breast cancer, cervical cancer, and bone density screenings. Women experience unique health issues and conditions, from pregnancy and menopause to gynecological conditions, such as uterine fibroids and pelvic floor disorders.

Women and men also have many of the same health problems. But these problems can affect women differently. For example,:

1. Women are more likely to die following a heart attack than men
2. Women are more likely to show signs of depression and anxiety than men
3. The effects of sexually transmitted diseases can be more serious in women
4. Osteoarthritis affects more women than men
5. Women are more likely to have urinary tract problems

Women's health needs to be front and centre - it often isn't, but it needs to be." - Cynthia Nixon

A woman's health reflects both her personal biology and her socio-cultural, economic and physical environment. These factors affect both the duration and quality of his life. For example, the average life expectancy of a woman varies greatly according to her caste. In 1997, the average life expectancy of white women was 5 years higher than that of African American women (80 years versus 75 years). Women who live in poverty or have less education than high school have a shorter life span; high rates of illness, injury, disability and death; and more limited access to high-quality health care services. Historically, women have also been the primary health care providers and health decision makers for their families. Nearly two-thirds of women polled in a recent national survey indicated that they alone were responsible for health care decisions within their family, and 83 percent had sole responsibility for financial decisions regarding their family's health. or shared responsibility. Women are also the primary caregivers for sick or disabled family members. Of the estimated 15 percent of Americans who are informal caregivers, an estimated 72 percent are women—many of them sandwiched between caring for a sick relative and taking care of their own children.

- Gynecological health and disorders affecting women include menstruation and menstrual irregularities; urinary tract health, including urinary incontinence and pelvic floor disorders; and such disorders as bacterial vaginosis,vaginitis, uterine fibroids, and vulvodynia.
- Pregnancy issues include pre-pregnancy care and prenatal care, pregnancy loss (miscarriage and stillbirth), preterm labor and premature birth, sudden infant death syndrome (SIDS), breastfeeding, and birth defects.
- Disorders related to infertility include uterine fibroids, polycystic ovary syndrome, endometriosis, and primary ovarian insufficiency.
- Other disorders and conditions that affect only women include Turner syndrome, Rett syndrome, and ovarian and cervical cancers.
- Issues related to women's overall health and wellness include violence against women, women with disabilities and their unique challenges, osteoporosis and bone health, and menopause.

PRIORITY WOMEN'S HEALTH ISSUES

Heart disease is the number one killer of women. Although it is typically viewed as a man's disease, more women actually die of heart disease each year than do men. On average, women develop heart disease later in life than do men. In addition, women are more likely to have other co-existing, chronic conditions that may mask their symptoms of heart disease than are men. Symptoms of a heart attack in women may also differ from those in men, which can lead to a misdiagnosis of the disease in women. Women who recover from a heart attack are more likely to have a stroke or to have another heart attack than are men. In fact, 42 percent of women die within a year following a heart attack compared to 24 percent of men.

A stroke is usually caused by a clot that stops the flow of blood to an area of the brain. Stroke can cause paralysis, loss of speech, and poor memory. Stroke is the third leading cause of death for women, and it kills more than twice as many women each year as breast cancer. It is the most common cause of adult disability in this country. Women account for 43 percent (or 240,000) of the 550,000 strokes that occur each year and 61 percent of stroke deaths (97,227 of 159,791 annual deaths).

COPD includes chronic bronchitis, emphysema, and asthmatic bronchitis, all of which obstruct airflow from the lungs. In 1997, COPD was the fourth leading cause of death among women, claiming the lives of 53,045. While death rates from COPD are much higher in men than in women, the rates for women have nearly doubled since 1979. The most rapid increases have occurred in women ages 75 and older.

Long considered a man's disease, HIV/AIDS is a public health problem among women. Fortunately, increased screening for HIV among reproductive-age women and more effective therapies to reduce perinatal transmission of HIV has been quite effective. They have contributed to the 75 percent decline in the proportion of infants diagnosed with perinatally acquired AIDS since 1993 The most common mode of HIV infection among adult and adolescent women is through heterosexual contact, followed by intravenous drug use. Significant gender differences are manifest throughout the course of the illness as well as in the mode of infection. These differences indicate the need for gender-sensitive treatment and prevention strategies to stem the spread of AIDS.

Autoimmune diseases arise when, for unknown reasons, a person's body declares war on itself, producing antibodies that attack healthy tissue. About 75 percent of autoimmune diseases occur in women, including systemic lupus erythematosus (SLE), Sjogren's syndrome, rheumatoid arthritis, scleroderma, diabetes Type I, multiple sclerosis, and autoimmune thyroid disease. When considered as individual conditions, autoimmune diseases are not very common. However, taken together as a group, they represent the fourth-largest cause of disability among women. These diseases remain misunderstood and misdiagnosed.

Some common health issues that affect millions of women each year

Premenstrual Dysphoric Disorder

PMDD, commonly mistaken for the less serious PMS, is a condition that causes severe anxiety, depression, discomfort, pain, and tension prior to menstruation. It is estimated that between 3 to 8 percent of women in their childbearing years experience PMDD. The premenstrual dysphoric disorder is a serious condition that can cause significant discomfort for a woman before her period. The depression that accompanies PMDD is often severe and, in some cases, debilitating.

Fertility issues

The latest report revealed that the fertility rate of Indians has come down by more than 50% from 4.97 to 2.3, it will be further reduced to 2.1 during 2025 to 30, 1.86 from 2045 to 50, and 1.78 from 2095 to 100. Currently, the infertility rate is 10 to 14% which is higher in urban areas where 1 out of 6 couples is affected. Various causes responsible for infertility in women are PCOS, contraception complications, abortion infections, STDs, post-partum infections, pelvic inflammatory diseases, etc. Lifestyle problems such as smoking, alcohol, consuming processed food, physical and emotional stress can also play a significant role in infertility. The problem of infertility can be treated with the help of an expert depending on the underlying cause. There are certain hormone tests, such as the FSH test, that your doctor might suggest to get a sneak peek into your condition.

Thyroid problems

Thyroid disease is twice as prevalent in women as in men and is common among women of child-bearing age (18-35 years). Women generally have hypothyroidism (low thyroid hormone levels), in which the metabolism slows down. Symptoms include weight gain, feeling sluggish and tired, etc. On the other side, high thyroid levels can also cause early onset of menopause, before 40 years or in the early 40s. Besides, pregnancy can raise the level of thyroid hormones in the blood, and almost 5% to 10% of women suffer from postpartum thyroiditis, which occurs within 1 year after giving birth.

Postpartum Depression

Postpartum depression occurs immediately or shortly after a woman gives birth. While it is normal for women to feel sad or even depressed after giving birth or experiencing a miscarriage, postpartum depression is severe and lasts for months. Even women who are excited about having a baby and have plenty of familial support can develop postpartum depression. It is important to remember that if you are experiencing the symptoms of postpartum depression, it does not mean you do not love your child. Mothers suffering from postpartum depression may have difficulty bonding to their newborn child and feel a sense of helplessness. This is common, but it is a serious issue that requires medical treatment.

Menopause

All women go through menopause, typically once they have passed through their childbearing years. Menopause simply means that the body's reproductive system is no longer in the phase where it releases eggs for fertilization or builds a home for a potential fetus in the uterine wall. The ovaries stop releasing eggs during menopause, so there is no reason for the uterus to collect or shed the lining of blood and mucous that results in menstrual flow. The average age of onset for menopause is 51, but some women go through the change much earlier or later. Menopause can also be forced by a procedure known as a hysterectomy, in which the entire uterus is removed for medical purposes. Menopause can also be induced through the use of hormones. Many perimenopausal and post-menopausal women choose to take hormone replacement therapy (HRT), which balances out hormonal changes to prevent a significant difference in mood, hair growth, weight, and libido. Some common symptoms of perimenopause and menopause included:

Breast cancer

Breast cancer is the second most important cause of cancer deaths among women. The latest global figures show that around half a million women die from breast cancer each year. Various risk factors involved are increasing age, family history, early onset of periods or menopause after 55 years, obesity, etc. Keep yourself educated regarding breast cancer self-examination.

Sexual health and bladder issues

Women should be concerned about their sexual as well as bladder health as they rapidly get affected by both sexually transmitted diseases (STDs) and urinary tract infections. It has been observed that the effect of an STD is more severe on women than on men. Although STDs often go untreated in women as symptoms are less noticeable or have higher chances of getting misdiagnosed with another condition, they have serious implications such as infertility in women. Apart from sexual health, women should take care of their personal hygiene. Women have a shorter urethra, which enables the bacteria to travel a smaller distance before they reach the bladder and start an infection. Hence, urinary tract problems, including infections and incontinence, are more common in women. It is advisable to not hesitate and talk to your healthcare professional.

Endometriosis

Endometriosis is a problem affecting a woman's uterus—the place where a baby grows when a woman is pregnant. Endometriosis is when the kind of tissue that normally lines the uterus grows somewhere else. It can grow on the ovaries, behind the uterus, on the bowels, or on the bladder. Rarely, it grows in other parts of the body. This "misplaced" tissue can cause pain, infertility, and very heavy periods. The pain is usually in the abdomen, lower back, or pelvic areas. Some women have no symptoms at all, and having trouble getting pregnant may be the first sign they have endometriosis.

Gynecologic Cancer

CDC provides information and educational materials for women and health care providers to raise awareness about the five main gynecologic cancers. Gynecologic cancer is any cancer that starts in a woman's reproductive organs. Gynecologic cancers begin in different places within a woman's pelvis, which is the area below the stomach and in between the hip bones.

- Cervical cancer begins in the cervix, which is the lower, narrow end of the uterus.
- Ovarian cancer begins in the ovaries, which are located on each side of the uterus.
- Uterine cancer begins in the uterus, the pear-shaped organ in a woman's pelvis where the baby grows when a woman is pregnant.
- Vaginal cancer begins in the vagina, which is the hollow, tube-like channel between the bottom of the uterus and the outside of the body.
- Vulvar cancer begins in the vulva, the outer part of the female genital organs.

HIV/AIDS

HIV is the human immunodeficiency virus. HIV affects specific cells of the immune system (called CD4 cells). Over time, HIV can destroy so many of these cells that the body can't fight off infection anymore. The human body cannot get rid of HIV—that means once a person has HIV, he or she has it for life. There is no cure at this time, but with proper medical care, the virus can be controlled. HIV is the virus that can lead to acquired immune deficiency syndrome or AIDS. AIDS is the late stage of HIV infection when a person's immune system is severely damaged.

- HIV in Women

Women who are infected with HIV typically get it by having sex with a man who is infected or by sharing needles with an infected person. Women of minority races/ethnicities are especially affected, and black or African American women are the most affected group.

- Pregnant Women

All pregnant women should know their HIV status. Pregnant women who are HIV-positive can work with their health care providers to ensure their babies do not contract HIV during pregnancy, delivery, or after delivery (through breast milk). It is possible for a mother to have HIV and not spread it to her baby, especially if she knows about her HIV status early and works with her health care provider to reduce the risk.

Interstitial Cystitis

Interstitial cystitis (IC) is a chronic bladder condition resulting in recurring discomfort or pain in the bladder or surrounding pelvic region. People with IC usually have inflamed or irritated bladder walls that can cause scarring and stiffening of the bladder. IC can affect anyone; however, it is more common in women than men. Some people have some or none of the following symptoms:

- Abdominal or pelvic mild discomfort.
- Frequent urination.
- A feeling of urgency to urinate.
- Feeling of abdominal or pelvic pressure.

- Tenderness.
- Intense pain in the bladder or pelvic region.
- Severe lower abdominal pain that intensifies as the urinary bladder fills or empties

Polycystic ovary syndrome

Polycystic ovary syndrome happens when a woman's ovaries or adrenal glands produce more male hormones than normal. One result is that cysts (fluid-filled sacs) develop on the ovaries. Women who are obese are more likely to have PCOS. Women with PCOS are at increased risk of developing diabetes and heart disease. Symptoms may include

- Infertility.
- Pelvic pain.
- Excess hair growth on the face, chest, stomach, thumbs, or toes.
- Baldness or thinning hair.
- Acne, oily skin, or dandruff.
- Patches of thickened dark brown or black skin.

Causes-Women's health disorders are caused by a variety of factors. Individual lifestyle, genetics, hormonal imbalances, age, and ethnicity can all play a role in which women's health disorders affect an individual woman. It is important to establish a relationship with a trusted general care physician who knows your family medical history in order to get a clear idea of which women's health issues you are most at risk for and learn how to prevent their onset.

Signs-The signs of a health disorder in females vary somewhat between individuals, but there are some common red flags to look out for. If you notice any significant changes in weight, the appearance of your hair and skin, mood shifts, or a change in sleeping habits, it is important to speak with your doctor. Heart disease is known as the silent killer of women because its symptoms often manifest much more subtly in women than they do in men.

Women's health involves a variety of gender-specific issues, like estrogen production, mental health, sexual health, and fertility concerns. Women go through dramatic mental and physical changes as their reproductive systems go through major changes. Women can take charge of their health by eating a proper diet, seeking the proper screenings, and maintaining a healthy lifestyle. While women are prone to many of the same health issues as men, there are certain issues that affect women exclusively or predominately. Disorders that exclusively affect women include menopause, postpartum depression, and premenstrual dysphoric disorder (PMDD). Women are also more likely to suffer from depression than men and for different reasons. It is important to understand these important women's health issues in order to take control of your own medical care. Preventative care is the best way to stay healthy, and by being aware of the signs and symptoms of women's health issues before they develop, you can stay healthy longer.

14

WOMEN AND MIGRATION: IN SEARCH OF BETTER AND SAFE LIFE

———❧———

The greatest good you can do for another
is not just share your riches,
but reveal to them their own.

Benjamin Disraeli

For the last few years, more female migrants have been migrating independently for work, education, and as heads of households. Despite these improvements, female migrants may still face stronger discrimination, are more vulnerable to mistreatment, and can experience double discrimination as both migrants and as women in their host country in comparison to male migrants. Nonetheless, male migrants are also exposed to vulnerabilities in the migration processes. Gender-responsive data on migration has the potential to promote greater equality and offer opportunities for disadvantaged groups.

Migrant women often play essential roles in sustaining and rebuilding their families and communities. According to the IOM women, migrants send a greater portion of their overseas earnings home than men do and they often take on more caring responsibilities related to family and household than men do – wherever they may be. The issue of violence against women is one all-too-common denominator underlying the distinctive challenges that female migrants face along the migration route. We must not forget that violence against women is a manifestation of deeply-rooted unequal power relations between men and women that we all must condemn.

Reasons migration is a feminist issue-

1. Almost half of the migrants are women and girls. And women are increasingly migrating alone or as heads of their households- Some of this movement is driven by conflict. Today, a record-high number of people have been forcibly displaced from their homes. It is estimated that about half of all refugees are female. Women and girls are also a significant proportion of economic migrants. They are the vast majority of all migrant domestic workers, for example. And women are increasingly migrating on their own, or as the heads of their households. This trend represents a key opportunity for their economic independence and empowerment.

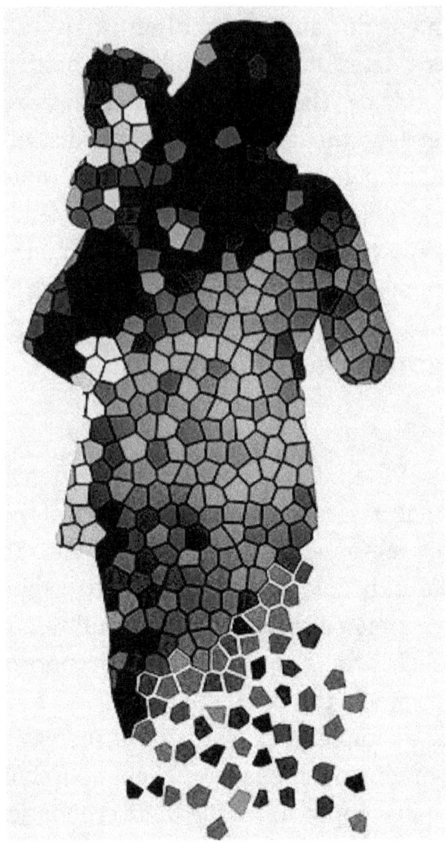

"You will never do anything in this world without courage. It is the greatest quality of the mind next to honor."~ Aristotle

1. Female migrants face major risks, including sexual exploitation, trafficking and violence-All migrants are vulnerable to abuse and exploitation, but female migrants are particularly at risk. Women and girls account for 71 per cent of all human trafficking victims, according to a 2016 report by the United Nations Office on Drugs and Crime. Women and girls also face additional vulnerabilities when they are displaced by conflict or natural

disaster. Chaos and the breakdown of protection systems mean perpetrators can abuse with impunity. Lack of shelter, overcrowding in camps and poorly lit public toilets all increase the risk of gender-based violence, including sexual violence. Families under extreme hardship may also adopt coping mechanisms that jeopardize women's and girls' welfare. A UNFPA-supported study, for instance, found alarming rates of child marriage among some vulnerable Syrian refugee populations.

2. Migrant women face double discrimination – as women and as migrants-Racism and xenophobia are serious concerns wherever large-scale migration takes place, and anti-immigrant sentiment is on the rise in many countries. Negative depictions of migrants and refugees often appear in the media, for instance, while the benefits migrants bring – such as their economic contributions – rarely make the news. Women and girls can suffer doubly from these attitudes, experiencing not only discrimination based on their migrant status but also based on based on their gender.

3. Women do not stop getting pregnant when they are on the move-Significant numbers of female migrants are likely to be pregnant or to become pregnant. While travelling – or in the chaos of displacement – women may lose access to sexual and reproductive health care, including family planning, antenatal services and safe childbirth care. Lack of these services can be deadly. In fact, it is considered one of the leading causes of death, disease and disability among displaced women and girls of childbearing age. Even so, migration may be a pregnant woman's best option in a crisis setting, especially if insecurity or collapsing health systems threaten her life at home.

4. Women and girl migrants are more likely to face health problems – both in transit and at their destinations.-Even after female migrants reach their intended destinations, they continue to face barriers to health care, especially sexual and reproductive health services. Foreign-born migrants can face significantly higher risks of maternal injury and death than

native-born women, for example, and higher risks of HIV infection, trauma and violence.**RECOMMENDATIONS**

- We observed a high proportion of women reporting economic reasons for their migration, indicating increasing feminization of migration for work opportunities. Thus, a well-organized support system for potential female migrants can facilitate their independent migration. Also, awareness campaigns at various levels would be helpful for the migrants for knowing the situation and types of work and facilities available at the destination. Migration information and support centers at some destination sites with high in-migration rates and at origin sites with high out-migration rates should be established.

- A shift from unemployment in areas of origin to informal sector jobs in urban destination areas was observed. This shift may be seen in the wider context of falling levels of economic security in rural areas. Although the implementation of the National Rural Employment Guaranty Scheme (NREGS) in many states of India has resulted in an overall increase in employment in rural areas and has decelerated the urbanization process to some extent, it is mostly benefitting men; there is a need to emphasize greater involvement of women in the workforce To reduce the pressure of migration to urban areas implementation of NREGA needs to be continuous and inclusive and linked to skill development in rural areas under the new national skill development program.

- Due to low educational levels and poor/nonexistent skill sets, a large number of migrant women engage in domestic work. While this may be a safer option as women work part-time in nearby high-income settlements, it may be worthwhile to establish centers to train these women in home-based income-generating activities like tailoring, handicrafts, or cottage industry. This would help in diversifying the available job opportunities for these women by an efficient allocation of skills leading to a more efficient labor market.

- Most of the studies' findings show a high prevalence of verbal and physical abuse of female migrants by their husbands. Since spousal abuse can often lead to poor physical and psychological health, the NGOs working in migrant settlement areas should organize peer support groups or one-on-one/couple counseling sessions to address spousal violence. If required, the NGOs should provide physical, mental, emotional, and legal support or referral to appropriate services.

- Certain groups of female migrants showed specific disease patterns. Anaemia, hypertension, and obesity were prevalent among the migrants in Mumbai. Diabetes was prevalent among female migrants in Delhi. Anemia was observed among more than half of female migrants. Although symptoms related to RTI/STI were commonly reported, treatment-seeking for these problems was low and unmet family planning needs were moderately high. This indicates the need for targeted IEC (Information Education and Communication) campaigns and behavior change interventions to create awareness about preventable diseases and to provide information on locally available low-cost public health care services. These interventions would benefit the larger community in these low-income high-density neighborhoods.

- Poor psychological health among the female migrants is also an area of concern, and there is a need to create awareness about common symptoms of psychological ailments such as depression and anxiety. This would enable these women to identify the symptoms and access necessary medical help without feeling stigmatized. Medical treatment for psychological disorders is available free of cost at most government tertiary care health facilities.

Around the world, more people are on the move than ever before. Many of them are seeking new opportunities and a better life for themselves and their families. Others are forced to move due to disaster or conflict. Gender is central to any discussion of

the causes and consequences of migration, whether ,forced, voluntary or somewhere in between. It is recognized that a person's sex, gender, gender identity and sexual orientation shape every stage of the migration experience. Gender influences reasons for migrating, who migrates and to where, how people migrate and the networks they use, opportunities and resources available at destinations, and relations with the country of origin. Risks, vulnerabilities and needs are also shaped in large part by one's gender, and often vary drastically for different groups. The roles, expectations, relationships, and power dynamics associated with being a man, woman, boy or girl, and whether one identifies as lesbian, gay, bisexual, transgender, and/or intersex (LGBTI), significantly affect all aspects of the migration process, and can also be affected in new ways by migration.

15

EDUCATION: AN INSTRUMENT FOR EMPOWERMENT

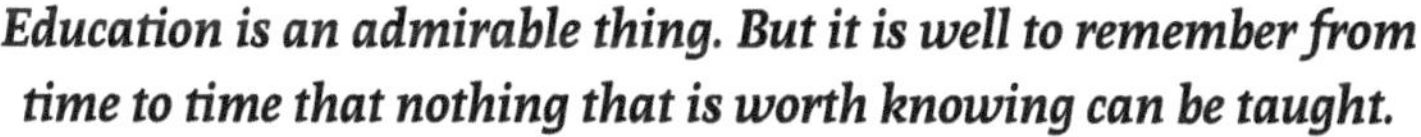

Education is an admirable thing. But it is well to remember from time to time that nothing that is worth knowing can be taught.

- Oscar Wilde

The Asian and Pacific Centre for women and Development defines [3]Empowerment as a process that aims at creating the conditions for self-determination of a particular people or group. Empowerment refers to enabling people to take charge of their own lives. For women, empowerment indicates the importance of increasing their power and taking control over decisions and issues that shape their lives. Literally to empower women is to give power to women. Delegation of power does not mean to feeling of superiority and dominance upon others. It is a sense of internal strength and confidence to face life. It facilitates for taking part in decision making and capacity building to contribute towards national development

India is a developing country in which poor and rich exist side by side and where the levels of poverty in the rural and urban areas are not the same. The problem that needs to be investigated in this study is that rural girls and women are suffering from poverty as a result of constraints that make them unable to continue with their education. In extremely poor societies girls' education is less prioritized due to financial constraints as well as the higher perceived rates of return to educating the male child than the female child. Failure of the female child to continue with school hinders her social and economic advancement. In order to break the poverty cycle, there is, therefore, a need to cast light on the importance of investing in female education. Female education has been the subject of a complex of debates. It takes into consideration areas of gender equality as well as access to education with the main goal of poverty alleviation. Education helps men and women claim their rights and also realize the potential that they have in the economic, political, and social arenas. Education is also one powerful and important weapon that fights and lifts people out of poverty as well as playing a role as a foundation for girls' development towards adult life. There are several arguments relating to the educational levels that need to be attained by an individual that is enough for poverty reduction. Colclough (2005) claims that the social returns of primary education are higher as compared to that of tertiary education in developing countries. This makes an argument for the provision of primary education on a large scale and making it free. However, King (2005) argues that universalizing and prioritizing primary education alone without giving adequate consideration to secondary and higher education, constrains development through a lack of necessary skills in administrative posts as well as in the management of the state.

The empowerment of women is directly linked with education. Women are the agents of change. Education is considered a key instrument for the change which is responsible for national development. It is true to the saying, "If you educate a boy you educate an individual, but if you educate a girl, you educate a family, society, and ultimately the nation". The National Policy on Education 1986 states, "Education will be used as an agent of basic change in the status of women. In order to neutralize the accumulated distortions of the past, there will be a well-conceived edge in favor of women.

"The roots of education are bitter, but the fruit is sweet."~ Aristotle

The National Education System will play a positive interventionist role in the empowerment of women. It will foster the development of new values through redesigned curricula, textbooks, training, and orientation of teachers, decision-makers, and administrators. The core of the concept of empowerment is the "idea of power" Empowerment is a multi-dimensional social process that helps people gain control over their own lives. Empowerment is an active and multidimensional process that enables women to realize their full identity and powers in all spheres of life. The empowerment of women is very much essential to achieve sustainable development. Education is the first step towards empowerment and the most crucial factor in over all development of individuals as well as the nation. Education is an effective instrument for social and economic development and national integration. Education enables women to understand their social and legal rights, become economically independent, acquire a voice in the affairs of the family and the community.

All over the world, gender inequality has been quite extreme. Studies have shown that inequality in education cripples the lives of millions of girls all over the world. Several scholars acknowledge that the gender gap has indeed narrowed over the past decade. However, girls are still at a disadvantage especially when it comes to higher secondary as well as tertiary education (Singh, 2006). The fate of most girls who would have failed to pursue their secondary education is to get married and bear children at a very young age perhaps to older polygamous or widowed men and some are forced into prostitution in order to make a living for themselves and their families (Khoo, 2010).

Njong (2010) maintains that investment in women's education is essential for poverty reduction, empowerment, and economic growth. There is an interrelationship that exists between education and poverty. "Education and health endowments of individuals are important components of human capital which make them productive and raise their standard of living or reduce poverty" (Barro, 2001). The higher the level of education of women, the fewer the number of poor individuals because it is documented that education impacts knowledge and skills supportive in higher wages (Talik, 1994). The Millennium Development Goals (MDGs) of the United Nations and the Poverty Reduction Strategy Papers have placed a focus upon primary education and the education of the girl child as a gateway out of poverty. The MDGs call for the elimination of gender disparities in primary and also secondary education by 2005 and to all levels of education no later than 2015 (United Nations Population Fund, 2003).

Nelson (2009) states that all over the world, there are more than 115 million children currently out of school and more than half of them are girls. Living in an environment of extreme poverty, rural women and girls in the poorest parts of Africa remain critically excluded from education and also economic opportunities. Njong (2010) asserts, "poverty may constitute a major constraint to educational attainment' through three possible means. First, poverty may handicap the acquisition. Second, poverty generates social pressures that influence the mindset of poor students. Third, uneducated women gain very little knowledge of family planning, basic nutrition, or even healthcare because it is almost impossible for these women in such marginalized traditional environments to acquire the important knowledge that has the ability to effect change (Bramley and Karley (2005).

Process of Women Empowerment

The process of women's empowerment results in a redistribution of power within societies and groups as well as between men and women. The attainment of women's empowerment is also contingent on the extent to which the humanness of women and girls including their right to self-determination and autonomy is recognized and respected and the extent to which changes in patriarchal structures and facilitated. The empowerment process is one where women begin to re-examine their lives critically and collectively. It enables women to look at old problems in new ways, analyze their environment and situation, and recognize their strength and their self-image. The process of empowerment enables women to access new information and knowledge, acquire new skills, and initiate action aimed at gaining greater control over resources of various kinds. Empowerment is not merely a change of mindset by a powerful demonstration of that change that the world around is forced to acknowledge. Armed with their growing strength, women begin to assert their right to control resources, including their bodies and participate equally in decisions within the family, community, and village. The process of empowerment has five dimensions.

1. The cognitive dimension refers to women having an understanding of the condition and causes of their subordination at the micro and macro levels. It involves making choices that may go against cultural expectations and norms;

2. The psychological dimension includes the belief that women can act at personal and societal levels to improve their individual realities and the society in which they live;

3. The economic component requires that women have access to, and control over, productive resources, thus ensuring some degree of financial autonomy. However she notes that changes in the economic balance of power do not necessarily alter traditional gender roles or norms;

4. The political element entails that women have the capability to analyze, organize and mobilize for social change; and

5. There is a physical element of gaining control over one's body and sexuality and the ability to protect oneself against sexual violence to the empowerment process.

Levels of Women Empowerment

a) Pre empowerment level b) Intra-personal (micro level) c) Interpersonal (mezzo level) d) Institutional (macro level)

Pre-empowerment level is the level of greater awareness about the prevailing system of subjugation of women in various realms of life. This awareness creates feelings of discontent which makes anyone to resist and to raise voice. At **intrapersonal level** the individual gains greater self-confidence and courage to resist exploitation and injustice practiced against them. At **interpersonal level** empowered women form a group and mutually reinforce their level of empowerment. Such groups gain collective strength to influence the society at large. At the **institutional level** the society as a whole decides to make institutional corrections to rectify the prevailing tender imbalances in both ideological as well as structural frameworks.

Education-A Tool for Empowerment

Education can be an effective tool for women's empowerment, the parameters of which are:

Enhancing self-esteem and self-confidence of women. · Developing ability to think critically. · Fostering decision-making and action through collective processes. · Ensuring equal participation in developmental processes. · Providing information, knowledge and information relating to their rights and entitlements in society with a view to enhance their participation on an equal footing in all areas.

Healthy, safe, educated, empowered women transform families, communities and countries. There is need to realize women empowerment firstly we will try to minimize the literacy gap between man and women, give priority to educate a women. Our former president Dr. A.P.J. Abdul Kalam rightly says, "Empowering women is a pre-requisite for creating a good nation, when women are empowered, society with stability is assured. Empowerment of women is essential as their thought and their value systems' lead to the development of a good family and ultimately a good nation". If a woman is aware of her rights, of herself, if her self - esteem is high, then she is empowered. But again when a woman is empowered, it does not necessarily mean that another individual becomes powerless or less powerful. On the contrary, if a woman is empowered, her competencies towards decision-making will surely influence her family's and neighbour's behaviour. Empowerment of women, therefore, needs to get utmost priority in any national planning process. As Swami Vivekananda said, "All nations have attained greatness by paying proper respect to women. That country and that nation which do not respect women have never become great, nor will ever be in future". The countries which realized the importance of empowering their women developed fast educating their women and is involving them in the decision-making process of social and economic development.

National policy for Empowerment of women came into force from 2001 which emphasizes:

1. **Creating an environment through positive economic and social policies for full development of women to enable them to realize their full potentialities.**
2. **The dejure and defacto enjoyment of all human rights and fundamental freedom by women on equal basis with men in all spheres-political, economic, social, cultural and civil.**
3. **Equal access to participation and decision making of women in social, political and economic life.**

4. **Equal access to women to health care, quality education at all levels, career and vocational guidance, employment and equal remuneration, occupational health and safety, social security and public office etc.**
5. **Strengthening legal systems aiming at elimination of all forms of discrimination against women.**
6. **Changing societal attitudes and community practices by active participation and involvement of both men and women.**
7. **Mainstreaming a gender perspective in the development process.**
8. **Elimination of discrimination and all form of violence against women and girl child.**
9. **Building and strengthening partnership with civil society, particularly womens organisations**

Education is a powerful weapon for empowerment of women. It is an investment in human capital. Education develops awareness among the women regarding their potentialities for active participation in restructuring the society. Realizing the key role of education in empowering the women several schemes have been launched. Under Sarva Siksha Abhiyan (Education for All) necessary steps have been initiated to reduce gender gaps.

(i) Early Child Care Education (ECCE) centres: These centres are playing a pivotal role in preschooling as it includes all children in the 3-6 age group. As the girl children usually look after the siblings they get deprived of primary education. But the ECCE centre facilitates the education of girl children. So that ultimately they get enrolled in primary education.

(ii) National Programme on Education for Girls at Elementary Level (NPEGEL): This programme is chalked out since 2003 to increase the enrolment rates of girls belonging to SC/ST category at elementary stage. It emphasises on enrolment, retention and quality education.

(iii) Kasturaba Gandhi BalikaVidyalaya (KGBV): This scheme is meant for girls belonging to the Scheduled Castes (SCs), Scheduled

Tribes (STs), Other Backward Classes (OBCs), religious minorities and below poverty line (BPL) households for bridging the gender gap. Those schools are opened to give chance to rural deprived girls to have their study upto or beyond class V.

(iv) Innovative scheme for the adolescent girls: This scheme intends to provide life skill education so that adolescent girls will be self confident.

(v) Mahila Samukhya (Education for womens Equality)

Even though education is considered to be a human right, unfortunately, women in some societies still lack access to this fundamental right. Studies show that girls are generally required to spend much more of their time on household chores than their male counterparts. Even when they are attending school, they are still expected to help out with household chores. Girls' labor is Studies show that girls are generally required to spend much more of their time on household chores than their male counterparts. Even when they are attending school, they are still expected to help out with household chores. Girls' labor is used to substitute for mothers' work and as such includes, caring for the siblings, preparing meals, fetching firewood and water as well as caring for animals and pounding grain (Oxaal, 1997). Such responsibilities do not align with the demands of education and this can hamper their achievement in schools and their possibility of continuing in education (Oxaal, 1997). In poor societies, families believe that men are a better investment and therefore women's education becomes minimized. The rates of returns to education are considered when there are financial constraints involved. Usually, girls' schooling is constrained when the perceived returns to female education are less than those for males. Parents from poor societies prioritize educating a male child because they believe the benefits are more tangible (Rose et al, 1997).

ppp

16

POLITICAL INCLUSION: STRUGGLE FOR POWER SHARING

———❦———

"We must have educated mothers. If a mother is educated, it is her first duty to treat the male and female child equally and in the same way, so that the girl does not develop a complex from the beginning."

<u>Begum Abida Ahmed</u>

Studies show higher numbers of women in parliament generally contribute to stronger attention to women's issues. Women's political participation is a fundamental prerequisite for gender equality and genuine democracy. It facilitates women's direct engagement in public decision-making and is a means of ensuring better accountability to women. Political accountability to women begins with increasing the number of women in decision-making positions, but it cannot stop there. What is required are gender-sensitive governance reforms that will make all elected officials more effective at promoting gender equality in public policy and ensuring their implementation. While numerous political advancements have occurred throughout the world in recent decades, the most important influence has to be on women's involvement and representation in political roles. Women make up about half of our population, but they are underrepresented in our political system in proportion to their numbers. At every level, from the home to the highest levels of government, women are excluded from decision-making. Women's decision-making engagement in politics may have a substantial impact on women's empowerment, which is why India is battling with the issue of gender disparity. Despite the Indian Constitution's provision of equal opportunity, women have a small presence in legislative bodies and political participation at all levels. Accessing the possible reasons, we see that, interestingly, education plays a part in politics; however, only for women because the literacy rate of female politicians is higher than the male politicians, implying that only women need political education.

Women's decision-making engagement in politics may have a substantial impact on women's empowerment, which is why India is battling with the issue of gender disparity.

India's failure with women's representation in politics isn't always appreciated internationally, perhaps because of a handful high profile women leaders commanding the headlines. Indira Gandhi was a famously hard-nosed prime minister and towered over India's politics for decades until her assassination in 1984. In contemporary times, Sonia Gandhi, president of the Congress party, or Mamata Banerjee, chief minister in West Bengal, are often touted as examples of women's empowerment. Majority of Indian women politicians are highly educated such as Nirmala Sitharaman, Finance Minister of India; Mamata Banerjee, Chief Minister of West Bengal; Mahua Moitra, an MP from West Bengal; Atishi Marlena, an MLA from Delhi; Mayawati, former Chief Minister of Uttar Pradesh. This fuels the notion that education does play an important role amongst women when it comes to political representation. The question of literacy not only restricts to contesting but also stretches to voting; to begin with, women's total engagement is low in states where female literacy is low and high in areas where female literacy is high. Furthermore, despite improvements in female literacy over the previous decade, female voter participation has remained relatively flat. It also important to note that no such link between men and literacy can be established. The disparities between overall voter participation and female voter participation are greater in states with low literacy rates. Males participate in the same proportions whether they are literate or not.

As per the report of the Election Commission of India, women represent 10.5 percent of the total members of the Parliament. The plight of women in the state assemblies is even worse, where they nearly account for 9 percent of the leaders. Women's representation in the Lok Sabha has not even grown by 10 percent in the last 75 years of independence. Women workers abound in India's main political parties, but they are often marginalized and refused a party ticket to run in elections. However, there are several factors responsible for the poor representation of women in Indian politics such as gender stereotypes, lack of political network, financial strains, unavailability of resources, etc. but one prominent factor that hinders the inclusion of women in politics is the lack of political education amongst women in the country.India's poor record on women's representation is starkly revealed by the World Economic Forum's Global Gender Gap Index 2021, where it has slipped 28 places, ranking 140 among 156 countries. India is the third-worst performer in South Asia, only ahead of Pakistan and Afghanistan, behind Bangladesh, Nepal, Sri Lanka, the Maldives and Bhutan. The biggest slump is in the political empowerment sub-index, where India ranks 51, dropping from 18 last year. The Women's Reservation Bill seeks to amend the constitution to set aside for women one-third of all seats in the Lok Sabha, India's lower house, as well as in all state legislatures. Yet the bill has languished despite passing the Rajya Sabha, India's upper house, in 2010, a delay described by one study as showing a "lack of seriousness among political parties in taking better account of women's increasing electoral participation".

Indian women have been subjected to widespread injustice historically and eradication of this injustice calls for one of history's biggest movements. It is saddening that the female gender continues to suffer discrimination and ferocity in diverse forms under polished labels. The Indian Constitution provides for universal adult suffrage — the right to vote for all adult citizens regardless of wealth, income, gender, social status, race, ethnicity, and political stance — to realize the true spirit of democracy. The equal right to vote proved to be one of the most liberating rights for women and a major bulwark against women stereotypes. Equal voting rights were not just limited to the 'Right to vote' but gradually led to participation in the decision-making process, political crusading, and political cognizance. The Constitution of India guarantees all Indian women equality under Article 14, prohibits discrimination by the State under Article 15 (1), assures equality of opportunity under Article 16 and mandates equal pay for equal work under Article 39 (d) and Article 42.

Indian politics has been witnessing a dramatic shift towards feminist politics over the past few years. They have come a long way from being an ornamental part of rallies to influencing the manifestos of political parties, making those more women-centric. The party manifestos are now recognizing even the unpaid household labor of women by assuring fixed monthly payments to women heads of households in certain states. Women in India are flourishing not only in social and political spheres but also in the economic sector. Although women in India have made remarkable progress and achievements in social, political, and economic spheres but getting down to brass tacks, most of this glorified progress and achievements are limited to some elite sections of society.

Women from all castes, communities, and religions in India belong to one category – women, so far discrimination is concerned. They are oppressed, ostracized, harassed, and victimized. However, the degree or forms may be varied. You cannot say that an economically independent woman does not face any form of direct or indirect violence or humiliation and is not given their due. Therefore, political inclusion is imperative. It is one of the platforms where, if proper representation is given it may provide opportunities to put forth their problems as women and also prove their worth. However, looking at the attitude of political parties towards.

The Women's Reservation Bill (108th Constitutional Amendment Bill, 9th March 2010) in Parliament seems a distant dream. (The Women's Reservation Bill or The Constitution (108th Amendment) Bill, 9th March 2010, is a pending bill in the Parliament of India which proposes to amend the Constitution of India to reserve 1/3rd of all seats in the Lower house of Parliament of India, the Lok Sabha, and in all state legislative assemblies for women). Several factors like demographic dividend, the stable political structure at the Centre, strong international relations, economic growth, global diaspora, advanced armed forces, etc. are jointly contributing India to transcend its way. But a dispassionate reality is that India can realize its true potential of demographic dividend only with gender inclusivity. The need of the hour is to invest in fostering gender dividends. Women participation has suffered for ages and looking at the grave circumstances we are in, these raw steps are nugatory, therefore, there is an urgent need for policies that can ensure better representation of women in the country such as more strict policies and implementation of girl-

child education in the country; initiatives from the recognised political parties to ensure that women receive a minimum agreed-upon representation in state assembly and parliamentary elections; passage of Women Reservation Bill; safe political space for women and debunking of the stereotyped role of women. Extrapolating these aspects, women's political participation in India still has a long way to go, particularly at greater levels of government. However, with more female political leaders and more women practising their democratic rights, we may expect policy changes that will help India improve its political performance.

17

WOMEN'S SAFETY IN CITYSCAPE: SECURING URBAN SPACES

Keep your eyes on the stars, and your feet on the ground.
We are what we repeatedly do.
Excellence, therefore, is not an act but a habit.

Aristotle

The rapid urbanization taking place the world over has opened up a whole new chapter of research, drawing linkages between political economy, social relations, safety, and communities. Alongside this wave of modernization that is sweeping the cities, there is an undercurrent of a deepening sense of isolation and increasing vulnerability of sections of society that have traditionally been at a disadvantage because of their gender, class, migrant status, age or sexual orientation. This vulnerability is manifest, most importantly, in the manner in which these groups are denied or are unable to access what the city has to offer, thereby affecting their quality of life in ways that compel them to negotiate their movements across the city even as they face pressures of all kinds. Among the many axes of discrimination and exclusion, gender occupies a central position. There are many factors that play a role in determining women's access to the city. The safety of women and gender-inclusive cities are broad concepts, but for this study the focus will be on the ability of women to participate in life in the city, to study, to work, and move around, and more specifically to address the violence that women and girls face in the process of carrying out their daily activities.

Gender-based violence is present at various levels, beginning with discrimination at birth, further perpetuated through discrimination in education, nutrition, employment, wages, and direct/indirect acts of sexual aggression. There have been several approaches to countering gender-based violence including campaigns, legislation, and institutional mechanisms. In the 70s and 80s, women's movements were at the forefront of a vibrant 'second wave of feminism', unleashing strident women's agitations against issues such as dowry-related violence and death, rape, and sexual assault.4 This phase was significant as it signaled to break the silence around violence against women (VAW) which led to several legal reforms including a comprehensive Prevention of Domestic Violence Act and one on Sexual Assault. A Bill on the Prevention of Sexual Harassment at the Workplace is also pending, though there is a Supreme Court judgment on the issue since 1992. There are also several sections of the Indian Penal Code that deal with sexual harassment.

The women's right to a public place is embedded in the concept of 'safety'. What is women's safety? It is largely referred to in the societal narratives and policy discourses as a condition wherein they are free of sexual assault and harassment; while for men, the term safety refers to being free of all types of violence (Desai, Parmar, & Mahadevia, 2017). Although women also experience robberies and road accidents and hence are not safe, the preoccupied notion of associating women's bodies with their families 'honor' makes their sexual safety of the utmost importance. Phadke (2007, p. 1512) argues:

DEFINING WOMEN'S SAFETY

1. Women's safety involves strategies, practices, and policies which aim to reduce gender-based violence (or violence against women), including women's fear of crime.

2. Women's safety involves safe spaces. Space is not neutral. Space that causes fear restricts movement and thus the community's use of the space. Lack of movement and comfort is a form of social exclusion. Conversely, space can also create a sensation of safety and comfort and can serve to discourage violence. Therefore planning and policy around safety should always involve and consider women.

3. Women's safety involves freedom from poverty. This includes safe access to water, the existence, and security of communal toilet facilities in informal settlements, slum upgrades, gender-sensitive street and city design, safe car parks, shopping centers, and public transportation.

4. Women's safety involves financial security and autonomy. Family income plays a powerful role in the cessation of battering. Resource accumulation and mobilization is a core strategies for coping with abusive relationships. Similarly, women's economic empowerment reduces their vulnerability to situations of violence as they become less dependent on men and better able to make their own decisions.

5. Women's safety involves self-worth. In safe homes and communities, women have the right to value themselves, to be empowered, to be respected, to be independent, to have their rights valued, to be loved, to have solidarity with other family and community members, and to be recognized as equal members in society.

6. Women's safety involves strategies and policies that take place before violence has occurred to prevent perpetration or victimization. This can happen by improving knowledge and attitudes that correspond to the origins of domestic or sexual violence, such as adherence to societal norms supportive of violence male superiority, and male sexual entitlement. Furthermore, women's and girls' full participation in

community life must be promoted, partnerships between local community organizations and local governments must be pursued, and including a full diversity of women and girls in local decision-making processes must be promoted. Prevention efforts involve strategic, long-term, comprehensive initiatives that address the risk and protective factors related to perpetration, victimization, and bystander behavior.

7. Women's safety means a safer, healthier community for everyone. This is a participatory process focused on changing community norms, patterns of social interaction, values, customs, and institutions in ways that will significantly improve the quality of life in a community for all of its members. This is a natural by-product of efforts that attempt to address issues such as family dynamics, relationships, poverty, racism, and/or ending sexual violence. Building a healthy, safe community is everyone's job.

The Sustainable Development Goals (SDGs) 5 and 11, as well as the New Urban Agenda, emphasize gender-equitable and safe, resilient, and inclusive cities. This implies women can enjoy city life in its fullest dimension as much as men. In other words, women have as much of a right to the city as men. Although the 'right to the city' is mediated by existing social inequities of class, religion, race, ethnicity, and caste in the Indian context (Kabeer, 1994), above all these equities are a layer of gender inequality. Gender refers to "culturally-mediated expectations and roles associated with masculinity and femininity" (Lips, 2015, p. 2). Gender roles are shaped by economic, cultural, and social norms and play a significant part in constructing unequal urban realities. Simply put, "women and men experience cities in different ways" (Beall, 1996, p. 10). Violence against Women (VAW), a global movement, captures how violence or the threat of violence against women fuels this differential experience. Another important aspect is the ability to 'loiter' in the city and seek pleasure without demonstrating a 'respectable purpose' (Phadke, Ranade, & Khan, 2009). While the forms of violence or its threat vary depending on social and political situations, these threats of violence, violence, and social stigma against purposeless loitering in the city are experienced by all women. Therefore, in this article, we use the term women and not gender.

"You will never do anything in this world without courage. It is the greatest quality of the mind next to honor."~ Aristotle

Violence against women is legally prohibited in many countries, the veil of superstition and cultural and age-old religious practices continue to violate women's rights. Women's constant exposure to various forms of violence in their daily lives reinforces gender inequality and curtails their mobility in cities and urban spaces. This 'daily' and 'normal' nature of violence or the fear of it often restricts or alters their interaction with the city. It also undermines their 'right to public space' and, consequently, their 'right to the city, understood as a state where every citizen has an equal right and access to the city and its public spaces (UNHABITAT, Department of Women and Child Development, Government of NCT of Delhi,

Jagori, & UN Women, 2010).

Literature on women's safety in India indicates that women are under the threat of different risks while accessing public spaces, even if they haven't experienced direct violence (Phadke, 2007, p. 1511): (i) potential physical assault, including the risk of life or injury causing physical or psychological trauma; (ii) risk of 'reputation', resulting in loss of matrimonial opportunity or questioning of sexual virtue (iii) risk of being blamed for being 'in the wrong place' or 'at the wrong time' (especially in cases of physical or sexual assault), resulting in the improbability of finding justice; (iv) risk of no or minimal interaction with the city, leading to a loss of opportunity and experiences. In case of any harassment, society often engages in victim-blaming (Sur, 2014), perpetuates that a potential act of violence annihilates a woman's 'virtue', instead of her 'autonomy', and teaches young girls to 'protect their virtue at all costs.' Therefore, women often hesitate to be in a public space without a 'legitimate' reason, as they are always looked upon as 'illegitimate' users of public spaces. Women feel the need to demonstrate their 'purpose' for being in public space and rarely tend to sit in a park by themselves or stand at a street corner, smoke, or simply watch the world go by like men do. Many activists, scholars, and feminists believe true women empowerment lies in enabling women to 'loiter' in the city as discussed above (Phadke et al., 2009). In the quest to create safe spaces for women, entry barriers are installed which, in effect, in a hierarchized society such as India, tends to exclude the 'undesirables', read men from low income and caste or men from other social segments. Thus, women's activists in India also emphasize that the public spaces cannot be made safe for women at the cost of anyone else's ('undesirable' sections of the society like lower-class men) freedom. Public spaces should be truly 'public'; they must be accessible to everyone throughout the day. Translated into public space terms, this means that the right of every citizen—across class, caste, gender, religion, and sexual orientation must be protected. The city can only belong to the women, when it belongs to everyone (Phadke,

2007).

Based on numerous studies (ActionAid International, 2013; UNHABITAT et al., 2010; Jagori, 2007, 2010; SAKHI, 2011; Women in Cities International, 2010a, 2010b) conducted in both the developed and the developing world, the built environment factors that affect women's perception of safety are:

1. Proper Lighting Dark street corners, entry/exit points, car parks, and poorly lit spaces cause discomfort to women during early mornings and late evenings, increasing the fear of violence. Women across the world have reported being willing to take longer or different routes to avoid such spots and stretches (UNHABITAT et al., 2010). Safety audits in Delhi highlighted that women felt unsafe in almost all carparks, which are generally poorly lit and are less visually accessible from the entry/exit points. This scares women from getting into their cars after dark (Vishwanath & Mehrotra, 2007, p. 1546). Conversely, women tend to use well-lit spaces or routes.

2. Empty/Dilapidated Building or Plots Women feel uncomfortable walking on streets with large empty walls or empty plots due to fear of not getting help in case of assault. Empty or dilapidated buildings are often favorable spots for men engaging in illicit activities, amplifying the fear of violence. In safety audits, the participants claimed to experience a greater fear of assault or rape in deserted spaces (Jagori, 2010, p. 17).

3. The extent of Oversight in Public Spaces Women prefers being in familiar areas, or in spaces where they can call for help or run away if they face violence or spaces that are active and eventful. Hence, it bothers them to be in spaces that make them invisible. "Together for women's safety" (UNHABITAT et al., 2010; Women in Cities International, 2010a) articulates the three major concerns of women in public spaces very well: to see and to be seen, to hear and to be heard, and to get away and get help. Different user groups like 'middle-aged people', 'older adults', 'women', 'families', 'familiar vendors & shopkeepers', etc. make

women feel more secure and safe (Jagori, 2011, p. 44).

4. Quality of Public Spaces Poorly-maintained spaces like broken sidewalks, unfixed potholes, open defecation, streetlights blocked by over-grown trees, etc. generate fear of violence, accidents, and health issues in women. Conversely, well-maintained and hygienic spaces make women, especially older or disabled women, feel safe. Wide, walkable sidewalks free of urinating men, cleaner spaces, shaded pathways, etc. increase convenience and safety in a public space.

5. Places with Visible and accessible Police Booths, Patrolling, CCTV Coverage, etc. As discussed previously, deserted and visually inaccessible spaces make women feel unsafe. Hence, spaces that are well-patrolled, have formal or informal surveillance or are close to emergency stations and police stations make women feel they can be heard and helped, and hence, safer (Jagori, 2011).

6. The extent of Familiar People/Shops/Vendors The presence of people, familiar shopkeepers, and vendors enhance informal surveillance in public spaces, making women feel safer. Plus, vendors and shops also ensure activity generation round-the-clock, ensuring more informal surveillance throughout the day (Vishwanath & Mehrotra, 2007, p. 1547).

7. Status of Public Toilets The inadequate public facilities make the lives of women from poorer/slum/resettlement areas acutely vulnerable. Public toilets in poor neighborhoods are often in a filthy and vandalized state, and hence unusable. Women have reported public toilets in those areas to be extremely unsafe as the male attendants often harass the women or frequently peek or break into the toilets. Men's and women's public toilets located close to each other increase instances of verbal and visual violence through the open roofs (Jagori, 2007; Parichiti, 2012), while the absence of toilets forces women to defecate in the open. To protect their modesty, women defecate in the open at night, falling victim to increased incidents of sexual harassment. Women report frequent encounters of flashing, staring, or stalking in these fields and public toilets (Vishwanath

& Mehrotra, 2008).

OTHER ISSUES

(a) Nowhere are the inequalities facing urban women more evident than in informal settlements where women account for over half the population. In these settlements, women face the most serious urban challenges: poverty; overcrowding, sexual harassment and assault, and lack of access to the security of tenure, water and sanitation, transport, and sexual and reproductive health services.

(b) Lack of secure tenure over housing and land affects millions of people across the world, but women face harsher deprivations. This translates into the situation that prevents women from buying land directly, having a house in their own name, or having control over decision-making regarding land and housing issues. There are negative consequences as a result of women's disempowerment over land and housing; it is women who are worst affected by evictions and by tenure insecurity caused by natural and human-made disasters, armed conflict, and civil strife. Thus, accessing, owning, and controlling land and housing empowers women to take control of their lives and to drive sustainable development and disaster resilience in their communities.

(c) Lack of safety and mobility is a serious obstacle to achieving gender equality in the city, as it limits the right of people to participate fully and freely as citizens in their communities. Poor urban design choices, such as poor street lighting and secluded underground walkways can make women more at risk of violence and sexual attacks in public spaces. Women's safety involves strategies, practices, and policies which aim to reduce gender-based violence, including women's vulnerability to crime. Making communities safer for all requires a change in community norms, patterns of social interaction, values, customs, and institutions. Thus, gender-sensitive policies, planning, and approaches to the prevention of crime and violence against women need to be inclusive of development and safety strategies.

(d) In the city, women have more opportunities for gainful employment; however, they continue to earn less than men for their labor. This is due to their concentration in lower-paid jobs, as well as, cultural and traditional patterns that result in their labor being valued less than that of men. Women living in poverty face immense challenges in accessing credit and financing for themselves and their organizations. Ensuring the integration of women to public life and jobs through the specific location of economic activities for market and accessible commercial uses, public venues, and other services, in which social and economic dimensions are developed, is shown to lower poverty levels. Finally, economic empowerment grants women more decision-making power within the family and is linked to lower levels of domestic violence and femicide.

(e) Lack of access to clean water, sanitation, and other basic services poses risks to health. Women, particularly those in poor urban communities, are at greater risk of experiencing health problems, since they are often prevented from accessing, and benefiting from, quality health services due to a lack of adequate services, systems, and socio-political will. Women are more likely than men to experience physical, sexual, and emotional violence, which adversely affects their health. Communities living in poverty carry the greatest HIV/AIDS burden compared to other urban groups. Socio-economic, cultural, and political power disparities; stigma, and the burden of unpaid care-work contribute to this imbalance. Therefore, urban programs must consider these disparities and inequalities as well as address patriarchal patterns of controlling women's sexuality and reproduction, so as to support sustainable community development and health systems that demonstrate results

Women feel insecure in public spaces due to multiple factors like poor design and infrastructure, society's behavioral pattern, shortcomings of the education system (towards gender relations, sexuality), and economic disparity. Apart from the built environment elements— like streetlights, state of sidewalks, maintenance of public spaces, dark/abandoned buildings or

areas, areas of visual or hearing isolation, etc.—the type of users and footfall largely affects women's perception of safety. Dhar (2013) states women feel safer with 'eyes on the street' (presence of people, vendors, drivers, etc.), a concept popularized by Jane Jacobs (1992) in the context of American neighborhood planning. Women in Delhi identified 'disrespect for women' as a major concern while using public transport: Girls and women who travel on RTVs (road transport vehicles/buses) face constant harassment from drivers, conductors, and their associates, who make vulgar comments, play loud suggestive songs, or crowd against women and push or rub against them. (Jagori, 2007, p. 36)

18

WOMEN AND MEDIA—THE DARKER SIDE

Sexism, as openly expressed as in those days, is not accepted anymore. There are many more female politicians and journalists as thirty years ago, I count my blessings. There are many more "roles" for women available now, as strong, powerful persons in every phase of our lives. Yet, is this reflected enough in the media? That is an important question for you.

Andrée van Es, Deputy Mayor of Amsterdam

Media has a significant impact on how social and cultural norms relating to women and to gender form and evolve. At the same time, women's image and the role that women play in the media are heavily influenced by existing social and cultural norms. The media's most important role has always been linked to that of a watchdog and informing the citizenry so that participation in public affairs and decisions can be realized through democratic deliberation. The underlying conditions of democratic, mediated public deliberation are equitable access to and exercise of citizenship rights, namely social, economic, cultural, and political rights. This means that public deliberation, at whose center the media are firmly anchored, can be democratic only when speakers, viewpoints, and experiences are accorded equal respect and space, and where equality of dialogue partners is guaranteed.

The early suffrage leaders needed the attention of the news media to carry their ideas and activities to the wider public, but male-run newspapers and magazines largely ignored the women activists. The news outlets that did cover women frequently trivialized their goals. Women who departed from the social norms of passivity and deference to male authority, and the traditional roles of wife and mother, risked being characterized as inappropriate, insane, or misfits. If they demanded equality with men, the media depicted them either as curiosities or as loud, militant, and aggressive. Such characterizations would continue into the early days of modern feminism (Epstein, 1978). Around the world, women are far less likely than men to be seen in the media. As subjects of stories, women only appear in a quarter of television, radio, and print news. In a 2015 report, women made up a mere 19% of experts featured in news stories and 37% of reporters telling stories globally. As behavioral scientists studying women's underrepresentation in the workplace, we know that this gender-imbalanced picture of society can reinforce and perpetuate harmful gender stereotypes. It is clear that the media must change how it reflects the world – but who can change media itself? For over two years, journalists and producers across the BBC have been tackling the gender representation issue by rethinking whom they put in front of the camera, with the goal of achieving 50:50 gender representation every month. "Outside Source"– Ros Atkins' nightly primetime news program that started the effort in 2017 — took its representation of on-air contributors from 39% women to 50% within four months. Today, 500 BBC shows and teams have joined the so-called 50:50 Project. In April 2019, 74% of the English-language programs that had been involved in 50:50 for a year or more reached 50%+ female contributors on their shows.

"The education and empowerment of women throughout the world cannot fail to result in a more caring, tolerant, just and peaceful life for all."— Aung San Suu Kyi, Daw Burmese-Myanmarese dissident and politician; Leader of National League for Democracy, Nobel Peace Prize Laureate

Not only were women's issues and leaders excluded from the media, but bias against women was practiced in reporting women's issues and leaders. Such treatment inspired women in many countries to establish their own magazines, newspapers and book publishing houses during the late 19th and early 20th centuries. The post-Civil War Woodhull & Claflin's Weekly had as its aim to make Victoria Woodhull the first woman president, while the Lily had a broad women's rights agenda, and the Una championed the rights of immigrant and poor women. Elizabeth Cady Stanton and Susan B. Anthony's short-lived but important newspaper the Revolution addressed a spectrum of issues related to women's discrimination, including low wages of working women and the right to vote.

By the late 20th century, women across the globe focused on enacting political and legal reforms to extend women's equality and access to social institutions and to ensure the protection of their rights. It was a new era for women's rights. Many women became politicized during independence movements, as countries broke from colonial powers. The legacy of that activism carried over into women's media like Ms. magazine, founded by U.S. feminists in the early 1970s; Manushi, an Indian feminist journal founded in the mid-1970s; and Isis International Bulletin, published first in Rome, then later in Manila. Another modern media concern was women's lack of access to media professions. Women were severely underrepresented in newsrooms, television and radio stations, film production and ownership of media outlets. More women on the inside, it was argued, would help resolve many of women's other problems with the media. Women such as Ann S. Moore (Time Inc.), profiled in this chapter, acknowledge the importance of women in their media operations.

Underrepresentation in news production arose through the U.N. Decade for Women (1976-1985), with leaders pushing the United Nations to fund women's news and feature services in the 1970s and 1980s to increase global news flow from progressive women's perspectives. They also gained funding for research on women and media and generated their own research. Two examples are the Brussels-based International Federation of Journalists and the World Association of Christian Communicators (WACC). The latter of these is among advocacy groups that sponsor research aimed at enabling strategy-building for women's equality in the media. WACC's (Canada) periodic study Who Makes the News? focuses on women's representation in news worldwide, while the International Women's Media Foundation (United States) conducts research on women's status in news organizations. IWMF also recognizes women journalists for courage in reporting with an annual "Courage in Journalism" award.

Stereotypes and media representations of women in different platforms have been studied a lot in the past years. However, much of the research can be either considered outdated or is very specific to a certain magazine or movie. Also, the studies made on effects of these media representations are mainly focused on how the stereotypical depictions affect women. Media representations of women leaders can affect the way girls and women see themselves in the workforce. Certain stereotypes and expectations can state the way they are expected to behave. Lämsä et. al (2002) summarize that a woman leader is mainly seen as a representative of her own gender while men are seen as 'neutral' leaders. Articles with interviews from female leaders often involve questions like 'How do you manage to both take care of the family and proceed in your career?' and 'Is it hard to be a woman in your industry?' (Eikhof et al., 2013; Lämsä et al., 2002). These type of questions asked only from female leaders can give people expectations of work-life and strengthen gender roles and/or stereotypes.

Coltrane and Adams (1997) concluded that women are more likely to be shown with their families, less likely to be shown in professional demanding jobs or leadership positions and more likely to be shown as sex objects. A couple of years later Ganahl et al. (2003) studied prime time commercials and found that many of these claims still apply - females were often cast as younger, supportive, and good-looking counterparts to men. Women usually have less dialogue and they are cast mostly to look pretty (ibid). Supporting Coltrane and Adams (1997) and Ganahl et al. (2003), Collins (2011) describes that women are often sexualized, including women in leading positions. Ganahl et al. (2003) stated that older females are the most underrepresented group in prime-time commercials.

These gender stereotypes are present not only among adults but among children, who are growing up in our society (Peruta & Power, 2017; Kahlenberg & Hein, 2010). Women and girls in television commercials targeted towards children are underrepresented in leadership roles and also overall (Peruta & Powers, 2017). While commercials are shown on children's television channel Nickelodeon featured girls in cooperative settings and with feminine toys, boys were portrayed in a variety of roles, most often outdoors and playing competitively (Kahlenberg & Hein, 2010). These stereotypes affect children's perspectives of gender roles –

their own and others' - later.

The role that media play in gender democracy has been of long-lasting concern when considering the process of moving towards gender equality. As things stand today, this role can be largely identified through two interrelated fronts. By representing and narrating gender and gender roles through content programming, design, and production, media shape and reinforce stereotypes and prejudices about women and men. These are also reinforced on a second front by the current structural organization of mass media and communications. The fact that women are still in a minority in media professions disadvantages them not only as producers of meaning but also as technologists and decision-makers. This persisting inequality has been the object of intensive and detailed studies for over four decades. Time and again, studies have shown that the numbers and proportion of women involved in the making of news, content, and the decision-making processes of media organizations are significantly lower than those of their male counterparts. This situation cuts across most professional positions, forms of media, news content, organization management, and so forth, with the exception of women's magazines. Studies have documented the existence of male dominance in media corporations, as well as a masculine organizational culture that has resisted change towards more equitable gender roles.

It is important to bear in mind that women are not a homogenous group with the exact same experiences, but they do experience what we call intersectionality: multiple and varying degrees of disadvantage and marginalization that may change from context to context, and from woman to woman. Yet these experiences are organized around the demographic markers of gender, age, class, sexual orientation, and physical and other disabilities. This element of intersectionality makes it difficult to talk about "women" in general, but it forces us to grasp the complexity of the challenges women face. It is also important to acknowledge that the aim for social change cannot focus on the "individual". It is not about improving the position of women in the media on an individual or even on a specific group basis, but about improving their position as a social group. Hence, although women are not just "one category", neither are they individuals devoid of social context.

Not only are female leaders presented in a different way than men, but their media coverage is also much smaller.

Media representations of women may affect the way women see themselves and their opportunities in their careers. As media images still portray men and women mostly in their traditional gender roles (e.g. Davis, 2003; Reichert & Carpenter, 2004; Peruta & Powers; 2017), the gendered images increase or help to maintain the current stereotypes in real life too. Representations of women in gender-stereotypical roles have been shown to activate gender stereotypes (Yoder et al., 2008). Gender equality is discussed a lot in the media these days, but the representations still tend to portray quite traditional gender roles and stereotypes on different platforms. As media continues to push these gendered media representations to people, it makes the present stereotypes in the society stronger, and they may affect people's decisions unconsciously. Even though gender equality in Western countries has taken big steps for the better over the past decades, women who make up half of the world's population are still very underrepresented in top leadership positions of political, private, and public sector organizations (Simon & Hoyt, 2012; Bligh et al., 2012). As media representations of women may affect our perceptions of women in the workplace (Cheryan et al., 2013; Eikhof et al., 2013; Simon & Hoyt, 2012), it is important to study these depictions and the effects they have. Changing these media representations may even help close the gender gap.

ԲԲԲ

19

WOMEN AND CYBER CRIME-RECENT THREAT FROM TECHNOLOGY

<hr>

'Honour is......what no man can give ye, and no one can take away.
"Honour is a man's gift to himself".
"Women are the heart of honour - and we cherish and protect it in them.
You must never mistreat a woman, or malign a man.
Or stand by and see another do so".

- Loren Klein

The computer-generated environment of the internet is referred to as cyberspace, and the rules that govern it are referred to as cyber laws. All users of this space are subject to these laws, as it carries a sort of global jurisdiction. Additionally, cyber law can be regarded as a branch of law that deals with legal issues arising from the use of networked information technology.

Cybercrime

Cybercrime is not specified in India's Information Technology Act 2000 or any other law. Under the Indian Penal Code, 1860, and a number of other statutes, crime or offence has been carefully defined by listing specific offences and their associated penalties. Thus, cyber-crime might be defined as a synthesis of crime and technology. To put it simply, 'any offence or crime that involves the use of a computer is a cyber-crime.' Cybercrime refers to crimes committed over the internet in which the perpetrator, hidden by the curtain of a computer screen, is not required to make personal contact with another person and may not always disclose their name. In a cyber-crime, the computer or the data is the target, the goal of the offence, or a tool used to commit another offence by providing the necessary inputs. All of these types of offences fall under the broader term of cybercrime.

Victims of cybercrime

Women and children, as the most vulnerable members of society, became easy targets for cybercriminals during the pandemic. During the pandemic, women, particularly housewives and those who are frequent social media users, were exposed to such crimes. According to the 2021 National Commission for Women's reports, the number of cybercrime incidents against women spikes during the lockdown time and then declines. In March 2021, the frequency of cybercrimes against women surged dramatically and continued to expand in April and May, when India was severely impacted by the second batch of covid-19, and nearly the entire country was subjected to stringent lockdown restrictions. Finally, as the second wave of pandemic subsided and lockdown limitations were lifted in June, the frequency of cyber-attack instances began to reduce as well and continued to decline in July as lockdown limits were lifted. The number of women victims of cybercrime was very low in previous years but surged considerably during the pandemic and shutdown.

Cybercrimes against women

People were forced to use the internet for educational, leisure, professional, and social purposes throughout the pandemic and lockdown. Working women began working from home using laptops, smartphones, and the web. Women who are still enrolled in school have been forced to use the web for online learning and other educational activities. Due to the fact that the majority of women were using social media websites and one or more online platforms for educational, occupational, and recreational purposes during this time period, the rate of cybercrime against women began to rise. Due to the fact that the entire country was on lockdown, criminals were unable to physically assault the victim, and thus began mentally and emotionally harassing them. The following are the most often encountered cybercrimes by women:

"Knowing yourself is the beginning of all wisdom." ~ Aristotle

- CYBER STALKING- It included contacting or attempting to engage with the victim via social networking sites or phone conversations despite her evident indifference, writing messages (often threatening) on the victim's page, and persistently pestering the victims with e – mails messages/phone calls, among other things.

- SEXTORTION- This is the most frequently committed cybercrime involving women during the pandemic period. The criminals began extorting or sexual favours from their victims by blackmailing them into disclosing their private photographs or modified images. By intimidating women, perpetrators sought sexual videoconferencing or letters from them in response to the pandemic frustration. Additionally, their lack of income emboldened them to extract money from victims by threatening them with their modified photographs.

- CYBER HACKING- People began reading news online during the pandemic. There has been an increase in the number of instances of bogus news and information. The women became victims of cyber hacking after clicking on malware URLs that downloaded all their personal information on their phones, activated the microphone and camera, and captured their intimate photos and videos. Offenders then utilize these pieces of data and images to commit sextortion and other crimes.

- CYBER-BULLYING- This would include posting false and misleading and abusive statements about the victims on social networking sites and demanding payment to have them removed, leaving hurtful comments on the victim's posts, exchanging morphed/private pictures of the victims without her consent, and sending rape and death threats to the victim, among other things. A sort of harassment and bullying is committed through digital or communicative devices such as a computer, mobile phone, or laptop.

- PHISHING- To earn money during the lockdown, criminals send bogus email messages with a link to a specific webpage in order to trick the victim into entering personal information such as bank payment information, contact information, and passcodes or with the intention of infecting the victim's device with harmful viruses as soon as the link is opened. These emails and texts look to be real. The perpetrators then utilize the victim's bank account and other private details to conduct suspicious transactions from the victim's account to their own.

- PORNOGRAPHY- Throughout the epidemic, perpetrators engaged in online sexual assault of women, morphing the victim's image and utilizing it for pornographic purposes.
- CYBERSEX TRAFFICKING- In contrast to sex trafficking, the victims have no direct interaction with the abuser. Cybersex trafficking occurs when a dealer broadcasts, records, or photographs the victim doing sexual/intimate actions from a central place and then sells the material on the internet to sexual abusers and purchasers. The offenders have sexually abused women by coercing, manipulating, and blackmailing them into becoming involved in cybersex trafficking.

Legal provisions

Although a full regulatory framework for laws regulating the cyber domain, including such activities, has not been drafted, certain legal remedies under various statutes can assist victims of cyber violence.

The Indian Penal Code 1860

Prior to 2013, there was no law specifically addressing online abuse or crimes against women in cyberspace. Section 354A of the 2013 Criminal Amendment Act amends the Indian Penal Code, 1860 by adding Sections 354A to 354D.

1. Section 354A: A man who commits any of the following events – a demand or plea for sexual services; or displaying pornography against a woman's will; or making sexual remarks – commits sexual harassment and may be penalized with stringent imprisonment for a period up to 3 years, or with a fine, or with both. In the instance of the first two, and with a period of imprisonment for a period of up to one year, or by a fine, or with the both.

2. Section 354C defines 'voyeurism' as the act of photographing and/or publishing a picture of a woman engaged in a private act without her consent. To qualify as 'Voyeurism,' the conditions must be such that the lady would "typically expect not to be seen, either by the offender or by any person acting at the perpetrator's direction." A person convicted underneath this section faces a fine and up to three years in prison on the first conviction and 7 years on successive convictions.

3. Section 354D added a stalking prohibition that includes online stalking. Stalking is described as an act in which a male pursues or contacts a woman despite the woman's evident disinterest in such contact, or watches a woman's cyber activity or usage of the Web or electronic communication. A man convicted of stalking faces up to three years in prison and a fine for the first offence, and up to five years in prison and a fine for successive convictions.

Apart from the specific revisions to the Code, there are a number of other laws within which cyber-attacks may be reported and the accused prosecuted. These include the following:-

Section 499: To slander, someone is to commit an act with the goal of slandering their reputation. When committed with the intent to injure the woman's reputation, defamation through the publishing of immediate and clear representation of imputation is punished with imprisonment for a period not exceeding two years, a fine, or both.

Section 503: Threats to harm a person's reputation, either to cause her panic or to compel her to modify her course of conduct about whatever she would normally do/not do, constitute criminal intimidation. The act of cyber-blackmailing a person, as was done in the aforementioned example, can be placed within the range of this law.

Section 507: This section establishes the maximum penalty for Criminal Intimidation committed by an individual whose identity is unknown to the victim. Any anonymous communication that constitutes criminal intimidation in violation of the preceding Section 503 is penalized under this section.

Section 509: Any individual who utters a word, makes a sound or gesture, or displays an object with the intent that such word, sound, gesture, or object is heard or seen by a female and insults her modesty, or intrudes on her privacy, maybe charged underneath this section and sentenced to up to three years in prison and a fine. This section may penalize instances of sexual remarks or comments made over the Net, as well as other explicit photos and content that are forcibly transmitted over the web.

The Information Technology Act 2000

- Section 66C– Identity theft is a punished offence under Section 66C of the IT Act. This clause would apply to instances of cyber hacking. Under this provision, anyone who uses another person's electronic signature, password, or other unique identifying feature fraudulently or dishonestly faces up to three years in prison and a fine of up to Rs. one lakh.
- Section 66E deals with a person's right to privacy being violated. Capturing, publishing, or sending an image of a person's private area without her agreement, or in circumstances that violate her privacy, is penalized by up to three years in prison and/or a fine.
- Section 67 makes it illegal to publish, transmit, or cause the distribution of obscene content and punishes violators with up to three years in prison and a fine on the first conviction and up to five years in prison and a fine on the second conviction.
- Section 67A makes the publishing, transmission, or facilitating the transfer of sexually explicit content a misdemeanour punishable by up to five years in jail and a fine on the first offence, and up to seven years in prison and a fine on the second conviction.

Indecent Representation of Women Bill 2012

This Bill controls and forbids obscene representation of women in advertising, publishing, and other forms of media. This Bill intends to widen the law's reach to encompass audiovisual media and electronic materials, as well as dissemination of material via the Web and the depiction of women on the web. But this Bill has been withdrawn in July 2021.

Particularly in an increasingly technologically reliant world, criminality related to electronic law-breaking is certain to increase, and legislators must go the extra mile to keep impostors at bay. Technology is often a double-edged sword that can be employed for either good or evil purposes. To combat cybercrime against women, the Legal system has enacted a number of legislation. Thus, it should be the relentless efforts of rulers and legislators to assure that technology advances in a healthier way and is employed for legal and ethical economic growth rather than criminal activity.

20

RIGHTS OF WOMEN — THE LEGAL FRAMEWORK AND CONSTITUTIONAL PROVISIONS

The day will come when,
after harnessing space,
the winds, the tides and gravitation,
we shall harness for Good the energies
of love. And on that day, for the second
time in the history of the world,
we shall have discovered fire.

Teilhard de Chardin

Human right is a global phenomenon. In view of the growing concern in the country and abroad about the issues relating to human rights to the changing social realities and emerging trends in the nature of crime and violence, the government of India considered it essential to review the existing laws and procedures. For better protection of human rights, the government has set up a National Commission under an Act of Parliament in 1993. When we deliberate on the topic "Women and Human Rights" what comes uppermost in the mind is the issue of human dignity. The rights relating to life, liberty, and equality are not less important or less valuable. In our democratic state every citizen, man, or woman is governed by the constitution. Gandhiji as early as 1931 made it clear that he visualized an India in which women enjoy the same rights as men. There is the perceptible vibration of the Gandhian concept of independent India as well as the other provisions of the constitution. The preamble embodies the spirit of the constitution, the determination to build up a new and independent nation ensuring the triumphs of justice, liberty, equality, and fraternity Equality signifies equality of status, the status of free individuals, and equality of opportunity. Equality of opportunity implies the availability of opportunity to everyone to develop his or her potential capacities.

"More countries have understood that women's equality is a prerequisite for development."— Kofi Annan, 7th Secretary-

General of the United Nations, 2001 Nobel Peace Prize winner

With the dawn of Independence, our constitution guaranteed equality to the genders. This was a great boon to the women of India, who constituted almost half of the population. What is demanded is not charity nor grace nor as legal aid to the weaker sex. The militant claim is the woman's right to be oneself, not a doll to please, nor an inmate of a workhouse. She has the human right to be a woman. The voice of women from the Kitchen is beginning to be heard at national and international fora. Even then, she stands at the crossroads. Though she has proved her worth in society, she still suffers untold miseries silently dancing to the whims of man. Rajagopalachari once said, "Woman can do everything these days, except become a father: "Sri Ramakrishna once said," She creates, presents and destroys the world with a mere wink of Her wondrous eyes; she holds the world in her womb. "Women are the gatekeepers of the family and through it the nation. They are the nucleus of the most vital social institution called the family. No socio-political system can ignore their vital contribution in nation-building.

Woman's Rights - The principle of gender equality is enshrined in the Indian Constitution

The principle of gender equality is enshrined in the Indian Constitution in its Preamble, Fundamental Rights, Fundamental Duties and Directive Principles. The Constitution not only grants equality to women but also empowers the State to adopt measures of positive discrimination in favour of women. Within the framework of a democratic polity, our laws, development policies, plans and programmes have aimed at women's advancement in different spheres. India has also ratified various international conventions and human rights instruments committing to secure equal rights of women. Key among them is the ratification of the Convention on Elimination of All Forms of Discrimination Against Women (CEDAW) in 1993.

Constitutional Provisions

The Constitution of India not only grants equality to women but also empowers the State to adopt measures of positive discrimination in favour of women for neutralizing the cumulative socio-economic, education and political disadvantages faced by them. Fundamental Rights, among others, ensure equality before the law and equal protection of the law; prohibits discrimination against any citizen on grounds of religion, race, caste, sex or place of birth, and guarantee equality of opportunity to all citizens in matters relating to employment. Articles 14, 15, 15(3), 16, 39(a), 39(b), 39(c) and 42 of the Constitution are of specific importance in this regard.

Constitutional Privileges

- Equality before law for women (Article 14)
- The State not to discriminate against any citizen on grounds only of religion, race, caste, sex, place of birth or any of them (Article 15 (i))
- The State to make any special provision in favour of women and children (Article 15 (3))
- Equality of opportunity for all citizens in matters relating to employment or appointment to any office under the State (Article 16)
- The State to direct its policy towards securing for men and women equally the right to an adequate means of livelihood (Article 39(a)); and equal pay for equal work for both men and women (Article 39(d))
- To promote justice, on a basis of equal opportunity and to provide free legal aid by suitable legislation or scheme or in any other way to ensure that opportunities for securing justice are not denied to any citizen by reason of economic or other disabilities (Article 39 A)

- The State to make provision for securing just and humane conditions of work and for maternity relief (Article 42)
- The State to promote with special care the educational and economic interests of the weaker sections of the people and to protect them from social injustice and all forms of exploitation (Article 46)
- The State to raise the level of nutrition and the standard of living of its people (Article 47)
- To promote harmony and the spirit of common brotherhood amongst all the people of India and to renounce practices derogatory to the dignity of women (Article 51(A) (e))
- Not less than one-third (including the number of seats reserved for women belonging to the Scheduled Castes and the Scheduled Tribes) of the total number of seats to be filled by direct election in every Panchayat to be reserved for women and such seats to be allotted by rotation to different constituencies in a Panchayat (Article 243 D(3))
- Not less than one- third of the total number of offices of Chairpersons in the Panchayats at each level to be reserved for women (Article 243 D (4))
- Not less than one-third (including the number of seats reserved for women belonging to the Scheduled Castes and the Scheduled Tribes) of the total number of seats to be filled by direct election in every Municipality to be reserved for women and such seats to be allotted by rotation to different constituencies in a Municipality (Article 243 T (3))
- Reservation of offices of Chairpersons in Municipalities for the Scheduled Castes, the Scheduled Tribes and women in such manner as the legislature of a State may by law provide (Article 243 T (4)).

Legal Provisions

To uphold the Constitutional mandate, the State has enacted various legislative measures intended to ensure equal rights, to counter social discrimination and various forms of violence and atrocities and to provide support services, especially to working women. Although women may be victims of any of the crimes such as Murder, Robbery, Cheating etc, the crimes, which are directed specifically against women, are characterized as Crimes against Women. These are broadly classified under two categories.

(1) The Crimes Identified Under the Indian Penal Code (IPC)

- Rape (Sec. 376 IPC)
- Kidnapping & Abduction for different purposes (Sec. 363-373)
- Homicide for Dowry, Dowry Deaths or their attempts (Sec. 302/ 304-B IPC)
- Torture, both mental and physical (Sec. 498-A IPC)
- Molestation (Sec. 354 IPC)
- Sexual Harassment (Sec. 509 IPC)
- Importation of girls (up to 21 years of age)

(2) The Crimes identified under the Special Laws (SLL)

Although all laws are not gendered specific, the provisions of law affecting women significantly have been reviewed periodically and amendments carried out to keep pace with the emerging requirements. Some acts which have special provisions to safeguard women and their interests are:

- The Employees State Insurance Act, 1948
- The Plantation Labour Act, 1951
- The Family Courts Act, 1954
- The Special Marriage Act, 1954
- The Hindu Marriage Act, 1955
- The Hindu Succession Act, 1956 with amendment in 2005

- Immoral Traffic (Prevention) Act, 1956
- The Maternity Benefit Act, 1961 (Amended in 1995)
- Dowry Prohibition Act, 1961
- The Medical Termination of Pregnancy Act, 1971
- The Contract Labour (Regulation and Abolition) Act, 1976
- The Equal Remuneration Act, 1976
- The Prohibition of Child Marriage Act, 2006
- The Criminal Law (Amendment) Act, 1983
- The Factories (Amendment) Act, 1986
- Indecent Representation of Women (Prohibition) Act, 1986
- Commission of Sati (Prevention) Act, 1987
- The Protection of Women from Domestic Violence Act, 2005

(3) Special Initiatives For Women

(i) National Commission for Women

In January 1992, the Government set up this statutory body with a specific mandate to study and monitor all matters relating to the constitutional and legal safeguards provided for women, review the existing legislation to suggest amendments wherever necessary, etc.

(ii) Reservation for Women in Local Self-Government

The 73rd Constitutional Amendment Acts passed in 1992 by Parliament ensure one-third of the total seats for women in all elected offices in local bodies whether in rural areas or urban areas.

(iii) The National Plan of Action for the Girl Child (1991-2000)

The plan of action is to ensure the survival, protection and development of the girl child with the ultimate objective of building up a better future for the girl child.

(iv) National Policy for the Empowerment of Women, 2001

The Department of Women & Child Development in the Ministry of Human Resource Development has prepared a National Policy for the Empowerment of Women in the year 2001. The goal of this policy is to bring about the advancement, development and empowerment of women.

Every citizen is entitled to enjoy certain rights as a human being. The fundamental rights enshrined in the constitution guarantee these basic rights. Equality before the law and equal protection of the law is guaranteed under Articles 14 & 16. Article 21 guarantees the right to life, and personal liberties. Equality of opportunity, prohibiting discrimination on the ground of sex, is ensured. The state is required to direct the policies towards ensuring the citizens, men and women equally have the right to an adequate means of livelihood, that there is equal pay for equal work for both men and women. Apart from these constitutional safeguards, an exception to the general rule against discrimination is engrafted saving measures protective of or beneficial to women. For upholding the fundamental rights and democratic freedom an independent judiciary is also created. New schemes like Legal aid, Lok Adalat, public interest litigation have come into vogue with the basic idea of eliminating the delay in imparting justice and reducing litigation expenses.

Several welfare legislations have been brought into force to protect and promote the rights of women and redress their grievances. Society has no claim to be called a civilized society if it is unable to protect the weak within itself. Society has given women vis-a-vis men an inferior status in almost all matters. No data are needed to prove discrimination and inequalities against women. According to UNICEF publication - Progress of Nations (26.6.1994). The performance of India in promoting the status of girls and women remains weak. Female literacy is very low in comparison to other developing countries. The maternal mortality of rate is very high (1:45) which is evidence of the unequal status of women. According to a World Bank survey employed women are in agriculture is 86% and only 7% are in Industry and 7% are in service. So that is why the status of our Indian women is low.

ppp

Bibliography

1. White, A.; Castle, I.J.; Chen, C.; et al. Converging patterns of alcohol use and related outcomes among females and males in the United States, 2002 to 2012. Alcoholism: Clinical and Experimental Research 39:1712–1726, 2015. PMID: 26331879

2. Slade, T.; Chapman, C.; Swift, W.; et al. Birth cohort trends in the global epidemiology of alcohol use and alcohol-related harms in men and women: Systematic review and metaregression. BMJ Open 6(10):e011827, 2016. PMID: 27797998

3. Erol, A.; and Karpyak, V. Sex and gender-related differences in alcohol use and its consequences: Contemporary knowledge and future research considerations. Drug and Alcohol Dependence 156:1–13, 2015. PMID: 26371405

4. U.S. Department of Health and Human Services and U.S. Department of Agriculture. Dietary Guidelines for Americans, 2020–2025. 9th ed. Washington, DC: U.S. Government Printing Office, 2020, p. 29. Available at https://www.dietaryguidelines.gov/sites/default/files/2020-12/Dietary_G.... Accessed January 6, 2021.

5. Guy, J.; and Peters, M. Liver disease in women: The influence of gender on epidemiology, natural history, and patient outcomes. Gastroenterology & Hepatology 9(10):633–639, 2013. PMID: 24764777

6. Hommer, D.W. Male and female sensitivity to alcohol-induced brain damage. Alcohol Research & Health 27(2):181–185, 2003. PMID: 15303629

7. Jones, S.A.; Lueras, J.M.; and Nagel, B.J. Effects of binge drinking on the developing brain: Studies in humans. Alcohol Research: Current Reviews 39(1): 87–96, 2018. https://www.arcr.niaaa.nih.gov/arcr391/article10.htm. Accessed June 19, 2019.

8. Squeglia, L.M.; Schweinsburg, A.L.; Pulido, C.; et al. Adolescent binge drinking linked to abnormal spatial working memory brain activation: differential gender effects. Alcoholism: Clinical and Experimental Research 35(10):1831–1841, 2011. PMID: 21762178

9. Seo, S.; Beck, A.; Matthis, C.; et al. Risk profiles for heavy drinking in adolescence: Differential effects of gender. Addiction Biology. In press.

10. Hingson, R.; Zha, W.; Simons-Morton, B.; and White, A. Alcohol-induced blackouts as predictors of other drinking-related harms among emerging young adults. Alcoholism: Clinical and Experimental Research 40(4):776–784, 2016. PMID: 27012148

11. Shield, K.D.; Soerjomataram, I.; and Rehm, J. Alcohol use and breast cancer: A critical review. Alcoholism: Clinical and Experimental Research 40(6):1166–1181, 2016. PMID: 27130687

12. Li, C.I.; Chlebowski, R.T.; Freiberg, M.; et al. Alcohol consumption and risk of postmenopausal breast cancer by subtype: The Women's Health Initiative Observational Study. Journal of the National Cancer Institute 102(18):1422–1431, 2010. PMID: 20733117

13. Allen, N.E.; Beral, V.; Casabonne, D.; et al. Moderate alcohol intake and cancer incidence in women. Journal of the National Cancer Institute 101(5):296–305, 2009. PMID: 19244173

14. Jha, D.N, How Hindutva Historiography is Rooted in the Colonial View of Indian History, The Wire.

15. Chakravart, Uma, 'Beyond The Altekarian Paradigm:Towards a New Understanding of Gender Relations in Early Indian History', Social Scientist, Vol. 16, No. 8 (Aug., 1988), pp. 44-52

16. Chakravrti, Uma,'Conceptualising Brahmanical Patriarchy in Early India: Gender, Caste, Class and State', Economic and Political Weekly, Vol. 28, No. 14 (Apr. 3, 1993), pp. 579-585

17. Roy, K. Power of Gender and Gender of Power: Explorations in Early India. New Delhi: Oxford University Press, 2010

18. https://blog.ipleaders.in/female-workforce-concerns-and-laws/

19. https://www.unfpa.org/news/five-reasons-migration-feminist-issue

20. https://blog.ipleaders.in/everything-about-cybercrimes-against-women/

21. Alam Aniket, (Dec. 20, 2003), "Sex Selective Abortions-Spreading Tentacles in Rural Areas", The Hindu, Republication.

22. Aravamudan, Geeta,(2007), "Disappearing Daughters: the tragedy of Female Foeticide, Penguin India.

23. Bansal Satish, (2003)," Workshop on Female Foeticide and Trafficking Among Women: Effectiveness of PNDT Act (1994/1996)", International Union for Health Promotion and Education, Punjab Chapter.

24. Bongaarts J, Guilmoto CZ, (2015), "How many more missing women? Excess female mortality and prenatal sex selection, 1970–2050. Population Development Rev. Vol.41, pp.241-269.

25. Census of India, (2011),"Census India", Office of Registrar General & Census Commissioner, India, Ministry of Home Affairs, Government of India, New Delhi.

https://censusindia.gov.in/2011-common/census_data_2001.html and

https://censusindia.gov.in/

26. Census of India, (20011), "Census India- Population Enumeration Data (Final Population)", Office of Registrar General & Census Commissioner, India, Ministry of Home Affairs, Government of India, New Delhi.

http://www.censusindia.gov.in/2011census/population_enumeration.html and

https://censusindia.gov.in/

27. Deshpande J.D., D.B. Phalke, V.D. Phalke, (March 2009), "Prenatal Sex Determination: Issues and Concern", Pravara Medical Review, Vol.4, Issue.1, pp.4-6

https://www.researchgate.net/publication/44259926_PRENATAL_SEX_DETERMINATION_Issues_and_Concern

28. George N., (Tuesday, 19 December, 2006), "10 million fewer girls born in India", A Study at India News Portal, Sify.com.

29. Grech, V. and Mamo, J., (2014), "Gendercide- A Review of The Missing Women", Malta Medical Journal, Vol. 26, No.8, PP.11.

30. Gupta S.C., (2003-05), "A Research Report on The Theme of Current Status of 'Pre-birth Elimination of Females in Ludhiana District" conducted by Department of Health Education and Family Welfare, CMCH, under the aegis of the International Union for

Health Promotion and Education, Punjab Chapter.

31. India Today Cover Story, (April 28, 2015), "Indian Women: Yesterday, Today and Tomorrow".

https://www.indiatoday.in/magazine/cover-story/story/19760115-indian-women-yesterday-today-and-tomorrow-819610-2015-04-28

32. Janmejaya Samal,(2016 Apr-Jun), "The Unabated Female Feticide is Leading to Bride Crisis and Bride Trade in India", Journal of Family Medicine and Primary Care,vol. 5, No. 2, pp. 503–505.

https://www.researchgate.net/publication/309301154_The_unabated_female_feticide_is_leading_to_bride_crisis_and_bride_trade_in_India

33. Liverpool Layal, (August,19, 2020), "Millions of Missing Female Births Predicted in India in Next Decade"

https://www.newscientist.com/article/2252285-millions-of-missing-female-births-predicted-in-india-in-next-decade/

34. Mainstream(March,10, 2008), "In Celebration of Womanhood", Special Correspondent, Mainstream, Vol. XLVI, No.12.

https://www.mainstreamweekly.net/article575.html

35. MathewS., (Dec,2000), in "Anuvibha reporter (Special Issue), Ahimsa, Peacemaking, Conflict prevention and Management Proceedings and Presentations, Fourth International Conference on peace and Nonviolent Action (IV) ICPNA), New Delhi: Nov.,10-14,19

36. Mittal, P., Khanna, K., Khanagwal, V.P. and Paliwal, P.K., (2013), "Female Infanticide: The Innocence Murdered Again", Journal of Indian Academy of Forensic Medicine, Vol., 35, No. 2, pp. 181-183.

37. Murthy Raman, K.V., (22nd July, 2006), "Female foeticide in India". http://www.articlealley.com/article_74633_28.html

38. NFHS-2, (2000), "National Family Health Survey-2, 1998-99, India", International Institute for Population Sciences, Deonar, Mumbai-8, India, and ORC MACRO, Calverton, Maryland, USA. pp. 5-329.

39. NFHS-5, (December, 2020), "National Family Health Survey-5- 2019-20: Vital Statistics", prsindia.org/policy/ vital statics

40. Patel, A.B., (2013),"Crises in Female Existence: Female Foeticide and Infanticide in India", International Journal of Criminology and Sociological Theory,Vol. 6, No. 4, pp. 235-241.

41. Ramaswamy Pratibha, (March,2007),"Female Foeticide: A Legal Analysis,", S.C., Corporate Counsel, Bennett Coleman & Co. Ltd.

42. Saikia Nandita, Catherine Meh, et. al., (June,01, 2021), "Trends in missing females at birth in India from 1981 to 2016: analyses of 2·1 million birth histories in nationally representative surveys", Vol.9, Issue.6,

https://www.thelancet.com/journals/langlo/article/ PIIS2214-109X(21)00094-2/fulltext

43. Savanoor, Banashri, B., "Female Foeticide: Need to Change the Mindset of People".

https://www.legalserviceindia.co   m/article/l292-female-foeticide.html

44. Sen Amartya, (December,20,1990), "More than 100 Million Women are Missing", The New York Review.

https://www.nybooks.com/articles/1990/12/20/more-than-100-million-women-are-missing/

45. Sen, A. (2003), "A. Missing Women-Revisited: Reduction in Female Mortality has been Counterbalanced by Sex Selective Abortions", British Medical Journal, pp.1297-1298.

46. Sen. Gita.,Piroska Östlin,(2007),"A Photo essay highlighting the plight of women in different parts of Punjab by Ruhani Kaur" in the final report entitled "Unequal, Unfair, Ineffective and Inefficient Gender Inequity in Health:Why it Exist and How We Can Change It",WHO Commission on Social Determinants of Health and Women and Gender Equity Knowledge Networks, pp.55.

https://www.who.int/social_determinants/resources/ csdh_media/wgekn_final_report_07.pdf

47. Singh Hitaishi, (2004), "Impact of Information, Education and Communication on Reproductive & Child Health Programme for Women in U.P." Unpublished Doctoral research.

48. Shrivastava, P.K., (2014),"Female Infanticide in 19th-Century India: A Genocide?", Advances in Historical Studies, Vol.3,269-284.

49. Working group on the Girl Child, "A Girl's Right to Live: female foeticide and Girl Infanticide", Report presented at the Conference of NGOs with Consultative Status with the United Nations" NGO Committee on the status of Women, Geneva.

50.Tabie Sheida, (June, 2017), "Stopping female feticide in India: the failure and unintended consequence of ultrasound restriction", J Glob Health, 525 East 68th Street, Box-124, New York, NY10065, Vol.7, Issues-1

https://anesthesiology.weill.cornell.edu/publications/stopping-female-feticide-in-india-the-failure-and-unintended-consequence-of-ultrasound

51. Poem of Ute Indians, http://www.umerpasha.com/strangew.htm

52. The Indian Express, (August 31, 2020), "Selectiveabortion in India may lead to 6.8 million fewer girls being born by 2030: Study".

53. Manjrekar Nandini, Trupti Shah, (October,2015), "Unmitigated Grief? Challenges to the Campaign against Sex Selective Abortion in Contemporary Gujarat",

54. https://www.researchgate.net/publication/282972772_Unmitigated_griefChallenges_to_the_Campaign_against_Sex_Selectiv

55. UNO, (2019), "UN, World Population Prospects, 2019", United Nations,

56. UNODC, (2013), "Current Status of Victim Service Providers and Criminal Justice Actors in India on Anti-human Trafficking Country Assessment- 2013", United Nations Office on Drugs and Crime (UNODC), Vienna International Centre, Wagramer Strasse 5, A 1400 Vienna, Austria.

57. Vickery Michelle, Edwin van Teijlingen, (February,2018), "Female infanticide in India and its relevance to Nepal-Review Article", Journal of Manmohan Memorial Institute of Health Sciences (JMMIHS), Volume-3, Issue 1, pp. 79, 80

https://www.researchgate.net/publication/323072838_Female_infanticide_in_India_and_its_relevance_to_Nepal/link/5a831096aca272d6501c337c/download

58. WHO, (2011), "Preventing gender-biased sex selection: An interagency statement OHCHR, UNFPA, UNICEF, UN Women and WHO", World Health Organization, 20 Avenue Appia 20, 1211 Geneva 27, Switzerland.

https://www.unfpa.org/sites/default/files/resource-pdf/Preventing_genderbiased_sex_selection.pdf

59. Yadav, Mukesh, Alok Kumar, L, (2005), "Medical Termination of Pregnancy (Amendment) Act, 2002- An Answer to Mother's Health and 'Female Foeticide', JIAFM, Vol. 27, Issue.1,pp.1.

http://andssw1.and.nic.in/swc/depts/dhs/docs/PNDT/MTP-FAQ.pdf

60. Anna Bofill Levi, Rosa Maria Dumenjo Marti & Isabel Segura Soriano, "Women and the City," Manual of Recommendations for a Conception of Inhabited Environment from the Point of View of Gender. Fundacion Mari Aurelia Company.

61. Alicia Yon "Safer Cities for Women are Safer for Everyone," Habitat Debate, UN-Habitat (Sept. 2007, Vol. 13, #3), 9.

62. Mary Ellsberg & Lori Heise. "Researching Violence against Women: A Practical Guide for Researchers and Activists," World Health Organization & Program for Appropriate Technology in Health, 2005.

63. Morgan J. Curtis. "Engaging Communities in Sexual Violence Prevention; A Guidebook for Individuals and Organizations Engaging in Collaborative Prevention Work," Texas Association Against Sexual Assault.

64. David S. Lee, Lydia Guy, Brad Perry, Chad Keoni Sniffen & Stacy Alamo Mixson. "Sexual Violence Prevention," The Prevention Researcher, Vol 14 (2), April 2007.

65. Morgan J. Curtis. "Engaging Communities in Sexual Violence Prevention; A Guidebook for Individuals and Organizations Engaging in Collaborative Prevention Work," Texas Association Against Sexual Assault.

66. ActionAid International. (2013). Women and the City II: Combating violence against women and girls in urban public spaces: The role of public services. Johannesburg: ActionAid

International.

67.Beall, J. (1996). Participation in the city: where do women fit in? Gender and Development, 4(1), 9–16.

68.Desai, R. (2014). Municipal politics, court sympathy and housing rights: A post-mortem of displacement and resettlement under the Sabarmati Riverfront project (Working Paper, No. 23). Ahmedabad: Centre for Urban Equity, CEPT University.

69. Desai, R., Parmar, V., Mahadevia, D. (2017). Resettlement, mobility and women's safety in cities. IIC Quarterly, 43, 65–76.

70. Dhar, S. (2013). Mixed city spaces are safe city spaces. New Delhi: Women's Feature Service. Jacobs, J. (1992). The death and life of great American cities. New York: Vintage Books.

71. Jagori. (2007). Is this our city? Mapping safety for women in Delhi. Delhi: Jagori. Jagori. (2010). Understanding women safety: Towards a gender inclusive city. Delhi: Jagori. Kabeer, N. (1994). Reversed realities: Gender hierarchies in development thought. London: Verso. Lips, H. (2015). Gender: The basics. London: Routledge.

72. Mahadevia, D. (2014). Institutionalizing spaces for negotiations for the urban poor. In O. P. Mathur (Ed.), Inclusive urban planning: State of the urban poor report, 2013 (pp. 148–166). New Delhi: Ministry of Housing & Urban Poverty Alleviation, Government of India, and Oxford University Press.

73.Mahadevia, D., Desai, R., & Vyas, S. (2014). City profile: Ahmedabad (Working Paper, No. 26). Ahmedabad: Centre for Urban Equity, CEPT University.

74. Moser, C. O. N. (1993). Gender planning and development: Theory, practice and training. London: Routledge.

75.Parichiti. (2012). Report on the safety audits conducted in Dhakuria, Bagha Jatin and Ballygunge stations, Kolkata. Kolkata: Parichiti.

76. Phadke, S. (2005). You can be lonely in a crowd: The production of safety in Mumbai. Indian Journal of Gender Studies, 12(1), 41–62.

77. Phadke, S. (2007). Dangerous liaisons—Women and men: Risk and reputation in Mumbai. Economic and Political Weekly, April, 1510–1518.

78. Phadke, S., Ranade, S., & Khan, S. (2009). Why Loiter? Radical possibilities for gendered dissent. In M. Butcher & S. Velayutham (Eds.) Dissent and cultural resistance in Asia's cities (pp. 185–203). London and New York, NY: Routledge.

79. SAKHI. (2011). Are cities in Kerala safe for women? Research findings of the study conducted in Thiruvananthapuram and Kozhikode cities, Kerala 2009–11.

80. Thiruvananthapuram: SAKHI. Sur, P. (2014). Safety in the urban outdoors: Women negotiating fear of crime in the city of Kolkata. Journal of International Women's Studies, 15(4), 212–226. UN Human Rights. (1993).

81. Declaration on the elimination of violence against women. Retrieved from http://www.ohchr.org/EN/ProfessionalInterest/Pages/ViolenceAgainstWomen.aspx UNHABITAT, Department of Women and Child Development, Government of NCT of Delhi, Jagori, & UN Women. (2010).

82. A draft strategic framework for women's safety in Delhi, 2010. New Delhi: Jagori. UNHABITAT, Women in Cities International, SIDA, Huairou Commission, & CISCSA. (2008). The global assessment on women's safety. Nairobi: UNHABITAT. Retrieved from http://www.preventionweb.net/ files/ 13380_7380832AssesmentFinal1.pdf Vishwanath, K., & Mehrotra, S. T. (2007). 'hall we go out?' Women's safety in public spaces in Delhi. Economic and Political Weekly, April, 1542–1548.

83. Vishwanath, K., & Mehrotra, S. T. (2008). Safe in the city? Retrieved from http://www.india-seminar. com/2008/583/583_kalpana_and_surabhi.htm Women in Cities International. (2010a).

84. 226th Report, Law Commission of India, Proposal for the Inclusion of Acid Attacks as Specific Offences in the Indian Penal Code and a Law for Compensation for Victims of Crime 7 (July 2009).

85. Acid Violence as on www.acidviolence.org/index.php/acid-violence

86. 226th Report, Law Commission of India, Proposal for the Inclusion of Acid Attacks as Specific Offences in the Indian Penal Code and a Law for Compensation for Victims of Crime 7 (July 2009).

87. Afroza Anwary, Acid Violence and Medical Care in Bangladesh: Women's Activism as Carework, 17 Gender and Society 305, 306 (2003).

88. Acid violence as on www.acidviolence.org/index.php/acid-violence

89. Bipin Kumar (2009). Women empowerment and sustainable development. New Delhi, Regal Publications.

90. Deepali Bora (2010). Women Empowerment: Present and the Way Forward. Guwahati, Purbanchal Prakash Publishers.

91. Hemraj Meena (2011). Women empowerment and Self Help Groups: Gender Disparity & Democratic safety. Jaipur, Aadi Publications.

ppp

Dr. Jaya Bharti (Academician, Researcher and Counsellor) is working on the post of Assistant Professor of Psychology at A.N.D. N.N.M.M. College, Kanpur University. She is a Gold Medallist in B.A and M.A Psychology at University of Lucknow (Uttar Pradesh). She earned her Ph.D. degree also from University of Lucknow (Uttar Pradesh). Besides that she qualified the UGC-NET-JRF in Psychology. She is a former Junior Research Fellow and Senior Research Fellow in University of Lucknow during her Doctorate. She has published more than Fifty five articles and chapters in National and International Journals and edited books. She has authored more then 10 books and two edited books. She is also a certified Peer reviewer in International Journals of Health, Wellness, and Society, Common Ground Research Networks, University of Illinois Research Park and Elsevier Journal of Infectious Disease (IJID) and an active Advisory Board Member (Psychology) in Cambridge Scholar Publishing. Her special areas of interest are clinical, counseling, research methodology, personality and psychological testing. Author has participated in many National and International seminars and Educational conferences organized by different educational organizations and agencies. She is a active member of various professional Societies. She has also conducted various literary and cultural events and workshops at University level .She is deeply involved in the promotion of mental health services and education of girls.

You may reach author at: psychologistjaya@gmail.com

Dr. Hitaishi Singh, an Academician, Researcher, Education Planner, Administrator, and Trainer, is currently working as an Associate Professor, Department of Home Science with a specialization in extension and communication at A.N.D.N.N.M. Mahavidhyalaya, CSJM University, Kanpur. Throughout her academic journey, she has been meritorious and was a university rank holder in her Post graduation. She was awarded ICAR JRF for

P. G., UGC Teachers' Fellowship for Ph. D., and qualified UGC NET for Home Science. She has also extensively worked for social causes and has been engaged with national and international development agencies such as World Bank/ UNFPAprojects, Population .....literacy house, Lucknow, Mahila Samakhya, and MVESS, Lucknow on several research projects, training, report writing, and documentation assignments.She has vast experience of working for institutional development and academic administration as Dean I/C of College Home Science, Tura, Central Agricultural University, Imphal, Manipur, Northeast India.She has been part of curriculum and syllabus development team of B.Sc. Home Science at COHS, Tura, CAU, Imphal, and was a member of Curriculum Development Committee, Home Science (HEFS for class XI and XII), NCERT, New Delhi. She has experience of teaching, research, and extension work of more than 25 years and has also worked in the development sector in a World Bank project before taking teaching as a full-time permanent job. The editor has presented several papers in International and National Conferences, invited as an expert speaker in Conferences, convened Conferences, E - Seminars, E - symposiums, and written 03 books, published 24 papers in National Journals, Proceedings and contributed chapters in edited books.

You may reach the author at: singhhitaishi30@gmail.com